The Messie
Motivator

Other Books by Sandra Felton

Meditations for Messies
Messies Manual
Messie No More
Messies Superguide
Messies Calendar
When You Live with a Messie

The Messie Motivator

New Strategies to Restoring Order in Your Life and Home

Sandra Felton

Fleming H. Revell
A Division of Baker Book House
Grand Rapids, Michigan 49516

Published by Fleming H. Revell
a division of Baker Book House Company
P.O. Box 6287, Grand Rapids, MI 49516-6287

Previously published under the title *Messies 2*

New paperback edition published 1996

Fourth printing, August 1999

Printed in the United States of America

Library of Congress Cataloging-in-Publication Data

Felton, Sandra.
    [Messies 2]
    The messie motivator : new strategies to restoring order in your
life and home / Sandra Felton. -- New pbk. ed.
        p.   cm.
    Originally published under title: Messies 2. 1986.
    Includes bibliographical references.
    ISBN 0-8007-5608-8
    1. House cleaning.   2. Women--Time management. I. Title.
TX324.F439 1996
648' .5--dc20   96-8629

Unless otherwise indicated, Scripture quotations are from the King James Version of the Bible.

Scripture quotations identified NIV are from the HOLY BIBLE, NEW INTERNATIONAL VERSION®. NIV®. Copyright © 1973, 1978, 1984 by International Bible Society. Used by permission of Zondervan Publishing House. All rights reserved.

Scripture quotations identified NAS are from the New American Standard Bible, © the Lockman Foundation 1960, 1962, 1963, 1968, 1971, 1972, 1973, 1975, 1977.

Illustrations by Bob Badaracco

For current information about all releases from Baker Book House, visit our web site:
                    http://www.bakerbooks.com

TO Ivan

who loved me in spite of it all.

Appreciation

to Tina—who typed my creative (translate
        "disorganized") manuscript and kept
        a backup copy of it so I wouldn't
        have to worry about losing mine.

to Marie—whom I seek whenever I want my
        self-worth bolstered. Unknowingly
        she inspired this book.

CONTENTS

INTRODUCTION

The story is told of a South Sea islander with the unlikely name of Johnny Lingo who went to bargain for a bride. The father and mother of the girl he had chosen to marry were outside the hut waiting for the big occasion. Villagers, who knew of all the happenings in the village, gathered around to follow the negotiations. Some of the men murmured that Johnny was an accomplished bargainer and would undoubtedly get a good deal. The going price a groom had to pay for a bride was between two and five cows. The women often compared the prices they had brought. Those who had fetched five cows wanted it known. The bride-to-be was a very shy girl and just a shade short of homely. Embarrassed and fearing humiliation, she had, to her family's dismay, climbed a tree some distance away to watch the proceedings.

Johnny arrived and squatted before the girl's father in the South Seas fashion. When the greetings were finished, he promptly offered eight cows for his intended. *Eight* cows! The deal was quickly concluded. The bride was bought. She and Johnny were married and sailed away for their honeymoon on a neighboring island.

When they returned, the owner of the general store went to their hut to deliver a package that had arrived in their absence. Johnny had ordered a beautiful ornate hand mirror as a wedding gift for his bride. When Johnny and his bride came out of their hut to greet him, the storekeeper was amazed at the transformation in the woman. Gone was the shy, homely girl the villagers knew. In her place was a radiant beauty, basking in the confidence of her husband's love and esteem. Johnny gave his bride her gift.

After she had gone into the hut, the storekeeper remarked about the startling change he had seen in Johnny's wife.

"I have loved her since she was young," he said. "I have always wanted to marry her, but I knew she felt unworthy to be my bride. I bought her for eight cows so that she would know and all the village would know how valuable she is to me. That knowledge brought the change you see."

This book is the Johnny Lingo story. The change in your house will be permanent only when you know what a valuable person you are. People of our quality do not live in clutter, do not hurt or embarrass ourselves by living disorderly lives. We are not two-cow people or five-cow people. We are eight-cow people. When we fully know and accept this about ourselves, the change in our houses will come about naturally and permanently because it will come from the inside of us and be outwardly reflected in our surroundings. The war against disorder will be won at last.

I am an eight-cow woman—a wonderful, valuable, eight-cow woman. I want to shout it to the world, to let the whole village know I am worthy, I am valuable. And so are you!

The Messie
Motivator

Facing the Enemy

PART ONE

1

The Winds of War

We has met the enemy and it is us.
POGO

There's a wonderful wind blowing in your life. It is the wind of change and it brings the hope of a new spring of order and beauty, leaving behind the winter of clutter and disorder.

The wonderful thing about spring is that it happens so easily and so naturally. Winter loosens its grip and slips effortlessly away.

That is not the way it is going to be with your housekeeping problems. They will not go away automatically.

I've got bad news and good news for you.

The bad news is that you must do it. The good news is that you can.

Let's get some idea of just how bad this winter is. There are approximately 33 million Messies in the United States. Some are men; some are women. Some are adults; some are kids. But it is on the Messies who are adult women that the problem falls the hardest. The reason is that adult women are the recognized organizers of the world. This is true at home or in business. It is true of wives or of secretaries. If you are the "senior" adult woman of a group, you are expected to be the organizer.

Notice I did not say that senior adult women are the organizers because they are good at it. You may be good or you may be awful at organizing. The job of organizing is simply given to this group because they are "supposed" to do it. This position has some good points. The person in charge of organizing can make things go the way he, or in this case she, wants them to go. For an organized person, being the organizer is a position of power. Power gives a person strength and a feeling of well-being. We see this in the lives of our organized friends. The friend who proudly shows you around her immaculate house (even opening her closet doors to show the tidy rows of clothes, shoes, purses, and so on) is not doing it for your benefit primarily. You may indeed be fascinated, even flabbergasted, to see this incredible order. But the real reason she is showing you her organized house is to flex her organizational muscles—to reassure herself of her power. She is experiencing a surge of well-being, a lift, from "showing off" the order she has created. There is a certain magic of energy that comes from being in control. By showing you around, she is raising her energy level.

There is motivation there, too. When she feels that surge of strength and energy, she wants to continue keeping the house in order so that she will keep on feeling that strength, that power.

This is true at the office as well. When certain information is needed and you can reach out and produce it with efficiency, you get a surge of confidence. This kind of motivation works especially well if someone else, the boss maybe, is standing there waiting. You want to continue keeping things in order so that you can experience this success again.

But it is not necessary to have someone else "see" in order to get this power. Every time a housewife opens the door to her organized closet and every time the business man or woman reaches for and gets information efficiently, they assure themselves that they are powerful. They are in control.

Do you as a Messie wonder how some people keep up their motivation over the long haul? Many are motivated by this power principle. When they feel control slipping away, they automatically shift into high gear. They cannot stand to feel frustrated or embarrassed. They cannot stand to feel powerless. It's frightening to them and they won't have it!

The 33 million Messies in the country are missing out on this feeling of power. They feel powerless and frustrated because they cannot get control of the house. They feel embarrassed and humiliated because others see their impotence. They feel harassed and degraded because those who must live with them complain constantly about the clutter and disorganization they are forced to live in.

Women from all walks of life have written to me, eloquently expressing how it feels to be a Messie out of control. Those of you who are not Messies will not understand the emotions of those of us who are fighting the battle with disorder and losing. Perhaps you thought we Messies didn't care. How wrong you are. We care desperately.

"I was drowning in a sea of clutter and was becoming paralyzed, apathetic, and numb in an attempt to preserve my sanity!"

Doris, Oklahoma

"The last few years I have felt hopeless because of my disorganization."

Shelly, Colorado

"I'm tired of running around like a chicken with its head cut off."

Heather, Massachusetts

"I lived for years in near-desperation because of my housekeeping problems."

Dot, Washington

"I knew there was something wrong with me, that I was a failure as a person."

Lynn, Idaho

Living in the winter of messiness is a very severe problem.

"I have just been thinking about the humiliation and loss of self-respect we suffer as the result of a messy and disorganized life. It is so destructive."

Betty, California

"I have been in complete despair."

Lois, Illinois

If you are a Messie, you know how it feels. We long for success and power. Too often we get frustration and failure.

But the winds of hope are blowing; surely spring is on its way. Perhaps before it is over we may call the winds of war the winds of hope.

IT'S TIME TO DECLARE WAR WHEN . . .

You find a four-month-old dry cleaning receipt in a coat pocket; you don't remember what clothes you took in and what's worse, you haven't missed them.

Your mother-in-law has submitted pictures of your home to Ripley's Believe It or Not.

You sort and wash a bag of clothes you found in the basement—then realize they were the clothes you had set aside for the Goodwill.

Your collection of ceramic mice that you've been collecting since eighth grade has filled three knickknack shelves, two coffee tables, the top of the refrigerator, your baby's old crib, and half of the bottom drawer of the guest bedroom dresser.

Your husband has painted over the basement door the words from Dante's *Inferno*: *Lasciate ogni speranza, voi ch'entrato*— All hope abandon, ye who enter here.

THE AGONY OF DEFEAT—
SYMPTOMS OF A DEFEATED MESSIE

Embarrassment "You'll have to excuse the mess. I, uh, well, the U.S. Olympic Pillow-fighting team just had practice here, and I, uh, haven't quite . . . just push that aside . . . well as you can see, uh. . . ."

Humiliation You open the refrigerator and the cat jumps out.

Frustration "Always winter but never Christmas." The treadmill of knowing what should be done and beginning with good intentions—but never finishing. There is probably nothing more frustrating than not finishing.

Anxiety That nagging existence in which something is always lost, late, or spoiled. (Akin to the concept that anything you like is either illegal, immoral, or fattening.)

Powerlessness Sort of like having a Rolls-Royce with a dead battery—what's the point?

Harassment Daily bombardment by the needs of family, home, and self. A domestic version of the London Blitz: mostly annoying, but with the possibility of real disaster.

Out of Control Suddenly your life takes on *Alice in Wonderland* qualities—and you find yourself shouting, "Off with her head," at the neighbor's pet cocker spaniel.

Apathy That point where you say, "If you care so much, *you* clean it."

Lack of Confidence *"I'll* never get this house clean."

Lack of Hope "I'll *never* get this house clean."

Lack of Luster "I'll never get this house *clean.*"

2

The Thrill of Victory

Discipline is the soul of an army. It makes small numbers formidable, procures success to the weak, and esteem to all.

GEORGE WASHINGTON

The Messies Anonymous group was born so that Messies could gain support and comfort from one another. Living as a Messie is a lonely life. No Messie really talks about housekeeping, not with any depth anyway. The people who talk about their messy houses are the Cleanies. Cleanies are those whose houses are always immaculate, except, perhaps, the rug has not been recently shampooed. With few exceptions, Messies suffer alone. Many, many Messies think, as I did, that they are the only ones who are having these strange, unexplainable problems with housekeeping.

Let me share with you their feelings. Since Messies Anonymous really is "anonymous," I will use only the first name and state. Some Messies would not care if they were known worldwide. Others might. Therefore, the anonymity.

"I don't feel quite so alone knowing that I'm not the only person who has this problem."

Regina, Delaware

"My first reaction was relief that there are others like me around (I always thought I was unique!)."

Betsy, Pennsylvania

I guess I should have known that others were having the same problem with organization that I was having, but somehow I must have tuned out the problems I saw in the houses of other people. I guess I thought their problems were temporary and surface. I knew mine were permanent and went down deep into the recesses of the bottom drawer of the most remote dresser.

Other Messies were not fooled as I was. They had other reasons for feeling that no one could understand their problem.

"I have been embarrassed, frustrated, disappointed, and ashamed. I knew I wasn't the only bad housekeeper in the world, but I thought most of the others I knew were just lazy. Not me—I worked from daylight till dark and never got the house clean. It was a relief to find that there were others like me."

Martha, Texas

Now, right here, before I continue telling you about members of Messies Anonymous, let's back up to explain how I discovered all of these fellow Messies.

Messies, as you must know by now, are those people who daily struggle with and fail at the important job of building the base from which they and their families work—their homes, or more specifically, their houses. They are not lazy. By now you know that they are not content with things "that way." On the whole, they show remarkable strength and good humor considering the ordeal under which they chronically live. Within each Messie lies a dormant pile of enthusiasm just waiting to be ignited by a spark of hope.

If you have not already guessed, I also want you to know

that I am a Messie. For twenty-three years I lived with the same frustration my fellow Messies have been living with. Finally I found a method that worked—really, wonderfully worked—for me. So great was my delight that I put a little ad in a local paper, advertising a class to share the program that helped me. Because I was a school teacher, this way of sharing came naturally to me. Because I was not really convinced that there were other Messies like me who would come to the class, I had some friends come sit with me at the appointed time and place. To my delight and surprise, twelve Messies arrived upon the scene. They were kindred spirits in search of the secret of successful housekeeping.

This was the first Messies Anonymous group. The name says it all. The word *Messies* has sort of a funny ring to it showing that we have a sense of humor and an upbeat approach to the problem. *Anonymous* shows that although we are working in a positive way to overcome our problem, it is still a personal thing. We don't necessarily want to include in our confidence those who may not understand. The two names together indicate that there are a bunch of us who want to be identified together for support and comfort. We have a definite program and plan to change—the Messies Anonymous program.

I tried other more positive names; I really did try. Apparently, people who are Messies are not interested in skirting the truth. Names like Happy Homemakers, Homemakers Unlimited, Domestic Doers did not make a ripple. Messies Anonymous did; it made a big splash. People who are Messies, and don't want to be, are interested in plain talk. They want it told like it is. So Messies Anonymous was the name.

As news of M.A. spread across the country, thousands of letters poured in. It is from a few of these letters that I quote.

In response to this outcry for help, I wrote *The Messies Manual, The Procrastinator's Guide to Good Housekeeping. The Messies Manual* is must reading for any reforming Messie. It explains all the basics of the M.A. program. One of these basic parts is the Mount Vernon method. Briefly explained here, it is, like all good ideas, simple and effective.

The Mount Vernon method is the first step to organizing your home. One of the Cleanies I talked to some years ago in my desperate search for help, told me that on a visit to Mount Vernon she was so impressed with the maintenance that she made it a point to talk to the woman in charge of housekeeping. She asked the housekeeper about the method they used. The housekeeper responded that she directs her cleaners to start at the front door and work around the inside periphery of each room. They dust and wax from the time they come to work early in the day until it is time for the public to arrive. A few minutes before opening time the workers collect their boxes of cleaning supplies and leave. The next day they begin where they left off and keep going from room to room until it is time to leave again.

But it's easy to keep Mount Vernon clean. George isn't there to mess it up. We are not going to use this method for dusting and polishing. Basically, we will use it as a method for organizing—not cleaning. You may want to clean a little as you organize, but don't emphasize the cleaning part.

Let's begin at the front door. You start with the first piece of furniture you come to which has a nook, cranny, or drawer. This is where you begin. Then you go around the inside periphery of the house, cleaning out these kinds of places.

You begin by throwing away all the junk you have accumulated in that drawer. Put it in a throw-away box. And be serious about it. Don't keep the pen that only works half the time and the year-old calendar even if it does have nice pictures on it. Your freedom from clutter is more important than these things.

Be willing to take a risk that you may later want what you have discarded. Also, realize that it may cause temporary pain to throw something out. Remember, however, it also causes definite pain to keep it. Throwing it out is mild pain compared with the pain that comes from having to live helplessly with all the clutter that finds its way into our houses. An exhilarating feeling of freedom comes once you make the decision to take control of the house and actually start by beginning to throw out things.

You do not worry about cleaning walls, drapes, upholstery, and so on as you go. Basically, you organize each spot. Along with your "throw-away" box keep with you a "give-away" box and a "store-elsewhere" box.

When you have done enough for one day, stop, and start again tomorrow.

Don't overdo. This is a marathon, not a sprint. Don't wear yourself out. Pace yourself. Take a day off each week so you will have a break to look forward to. Reward yourself when you get over a big hurdle.

Make a list of several items you plan to do each day. There will probably be from three to seven jobs on your list. Each day do these before you begin the Mount Vernon method.

You'll find real control developing before you know it. Boy! What a relief!

This is the method I taught at that first class. It has remained the basic get-control method for Messies Anonymous.

As the organization grew, I held seminars around the country, taking the M.A. message to lots and lots of enthusiastic Messies. But the number I reached was only a drop in the bucket compared to the many, many more Messies who wanted and needed help. So the job of Messies Anonymous was to find out how to reach and help them in a way that really would make a difference—a permanent difference.

The amazing thing was that it worked. It worked for women who came to the seminars. It worked for women who bought *The Messies Manual* and read it alone in their homes, finding for the first time that others understood there were real reasons for their problems, and that there was real help available.

Just as I had been thrilled, they were too and wanted to share their delight. I received letter after letter:

I am beginning my Mount Vernon. While Mount Vernoning the living and dining room, I'm also repainting them in a lighter, brighter color. This may not be a recommended approach, but the painting and seeing the growing picture doubles my energy and enthusiasm.

I'm not yet where I want to be, but it's getting closer, and I'm getting excited. When I feel overwhelmed, I close my eyes and see where I'm headed. It's lovely.

I think I'm ready to face the world; well, at least close friends. Soon, the world.

Lynn, Idaho

I have my self-respect back again and so much confidence. My daughter-in-law came by unexpectedly about 7:15 this morning and everything was clean and in order. What a wonderful feeling! One month after I started, all I have left to do is one shelf in my hall closet and one in my pantry.

My family is delighted. In fact, I'm a star in my own home and everyone is so eager to do their part to keep everything clean.

I had gotten to the point where I never entertained anyone and when someone knocked at my door, I would block the door with my body so they couldn't see in.

This past holiday season I wouldn't have any of the dinners at my house because it would have involved too much cleaning, but next year will be different and wonderful.Now there is a whole new me.

Pat, Louisiana

I have truly enjoyed discovering your *Messies Manual*. I have been using it in my home for the past six months. Using your directions I have made dramatic improvements in the appearance and organization of my home.

Alice, Florida

3

New Recruits: Volunteers Not Draftees

It is not enough to fight. It is the spirit which we bring to the fight that decides the issue. It is morale that wins the victory.

GEORGE CATLETT MARSHALL

It takes a lot of courage to be willing to take full responsibility for the condition of things. It is much easier to insist that we are victims of some outside force. The fact that we are not naturally good at housekeeping, that our houses are too large or too small, that we have low energy levels, that we work long hours, that we live with messy people, does not prevent us from having the houses we dream of. Our houses look the way they do because we have given them permission to look that way.

You and I are people of infinite value. We are people of dignity. We are not slobs. We are not undeserving. We are super, wonderful people. Somewhere in our hearts we know this. If we did not know it, we would not strive so hard to excel. And we do excel! All of us are successful in many ways. Where we are successful depends to a large extent on how we think about success.

Let me tell you the story of two women, each of whom was striving for success in her own way.

Beth is a composite of the Messie who feels that her value lies in what she is able to contribute to the world around her. She collects mementos because she feels that it is her responsibility to preserve the past. She is intelligent. The stacks of books, newspapers, and magazines in her living room show her interest in ideas. Her hobby materials scattered about attest to her creativity. The bits and pieces of leftover craft materials indicate her frugality. She has no time to stay home and do housework because she is so much in demand to do things she has volunteered for outside the home. When she is home she plays with the children or helps them with their projects. The house reflects this, if you know what I mean.

Here we have a successful woman. Beth is intellectual, frugal, generous with her time and energy, aware of the importance of her heritage, and an attentive mother. She certainly is creative. She uses her creativity to prove that she is a worthwhile person. Her value is there for all to see the second they enter her house.

"Come on in! Excuse my mess! I've been doing ceramics all morning," Beth says, often calling attention to the confusion around her, almost proud of it. Sometimes it is canning all morning, sometimes it is painting, but always it is clutter.

Woe unto Beth if she decides to become an elementary school teacher, a Sunday school teacher, or a Scout leader. She goes at every project with gusto. Charts, song sheets, posters, flannel-graph materials, and flotsam and jetsam for some possible future project would take over the junk room, overflow onto the bedroom floor and maybe even onto the bed to be removed to the floor each night.

I will not mention the problems she would have if she ever decided to take up refunding and coupon collecting seriously. (As a Messie, I know I can never be an elementary school teacher or coupon collector. I have tried both and found they require a much higher level of organization than I am able to maintain. For me to attempt either one of these jobs would be like an alcoholic trying to be a bartender. Some Messies can handle these activities with a lot of effort. I found it was easier to seek alternatives.)

Beth feels that because she is able to do all of these things she is successful. But the people who live with Beth are very frustrated; they hate the clutter. They let her know it in no uncertain terms. The children hesitate to bring friends home. Beth is frustrated and hates the clutter, too. Even she doesn't understand why she doesn't change. No matter how often she tells herself that the house is not that important, she continues to be bothered by its condition. But she won't change because this clutter shows, however poorly, that she is an important and valuable person. Beth continues to work at all these tasks to prove how valuable she is. Perhaps if she felt her own sense of worth more strongly, she would not have to keep proving it to others and to herself. The bottom line is that somehow, in proving her worth, she lost her dignity.

I first noticed how like Beth I am in oil painting class. I found that when I got paint splotches all over me, I wore them with pride. I was a painter! When I teach school, I end up with yellow chalk on my skirt and blue ink from the overhead projector on my hand. I don't really mind. I am, after all, a teacher. These messes set me apart as special.

Karen is also a successful woman. She has a strong sense of dignity and feels that her self-worth is threatened if her dignity is threatened. She feels that her home is an important reflection of her inner worth. She plans for its beauty and order to speak graciously of her. For her, the house is not just a location in which she *does* things. She feels that the house is a very personal extension of herself. Where does she get this feeling?

We are all made in God's image. God is a God of order and beauty. Karen feels this push to beauty and order very strongly whether she puts it in those words or not—whether she believes in God or not. We were designed by Him to feel at peace when things are in order and to feel frustrated when they are out of control. Karen may do fewer activities than Beth because she realizes she can't do as much as Beth tries to do and still maintain the way of life that she insists on. Besides, Karen doesn't think that abundant activity is necessary or desirable. She doesn't feel she has to prove her worth by producing. The activities she does decide to tackle, she does in the same way she keeps her house—an orderly and deliberate way.

Both Beth and Karen are successful in ways that are im-

portant to them. Beth values creativity; Karen values beauty and order. But Beth's success is not satisfying. She and her family are frustrated. Unless Karen goes to an extreme and becomes obsessed with order, she and her family will have a strong base from which to do the work they feel is important to them.

Beth set out to live a certain way and she succeeded. That way of life brought her misery. She had not bargained for this. The thousands and thousands of letters I have received pour out the trouble this way of life has caused. But the Beths of this world keep on trying to live happily following the Messie lifestyle. Many will not change. It is painful to change. They are willing to lose every shred of dignity in order to hold on to the unsuccessful path to self-worth they have chosen. But without dignity, there is no true self-worth.

When it becomes more painful to live in a cluttered house than to change, success is on the way. But not until then.

Let me share with you the story of one Messie as it is told by her son, whom we will call Roy. As always, personal details have been changed.

For years my mom has been collecting things either for sentimental value, or because she might need them some day. Through the years, the whole family has tried in every way we knew to get her to let go of much of the "stuff" that she kept. When we were younger, we were always embarrassed to bring our friends home, and we rarely had company. Mom realizes that her house is a "mess" and is very embarrassed and insecure about it.

Through the years, she has gotten more depressed, has lost almost all self-worth, and has had many, many very painful experiences because of her pattern of thought and because of the methods that we used to try to change her. I don't believe that any of us ever meant to injure her; we always believed that we were trying to help her. But Mom's self-image is so damaged, and she is so set in her habits, that I had really given up all hope, and frankly felt that she would probably either go to her grave early or lose her sanity early because of the friction and incredibly low self-esteem.

You so perfectly described my mom. She *is* a very devout perfectionist. She goes to great lengths to keep her home "germ free" while piling papers and many potentially "useful" things around till she can't even use most of her cupboards and closets.

Roy's mom did not get into this mess primarily because of low self-esteem. When she first started, things seemed to be going well. She found comfort, pleasure, and a sense of personal value in her hurried, collecting, creative way of life. Soon both she and her family began to be frustrated. Things slowly got out of control. In order to regain the comfort and self-esteem we all need, she turned to past gratifiers—collecting and activities. Unnoticed, dignity slowly slipped away down the stream of her unordered way of life. When she and her family noticed it was gone, nobody knew where to find it.

Perhaps you recognize something of yourself in the story of Roy's mom. All of us do. In searching for personal value in things outside ourselves, we lose the sense of dignity within ourselves. But there are certain steps we can take to find that lost or misplaced sense of dignity.

4

Basic Training: Action Steps to Dignity

dig·ni·ty/dig·nət-ē *The quality or state of being worthy, honored, or esteemed.*

Losing our dignity is rarely the result of a cataclysmic event. Oh, there are major traumas that can result in a temporary loss of dignity. But a real sense of dignity and feeling of self-worth are lost only after months and years of chipping away. Land stripped of the trees and grasses necessary to secure and protect the earth will erode. Maybe not noticeably at first, but after one or two years without protection, the topsoil is completely washed away and the soil becomes ugly and unable to nurture growth. Dignity is like the earth—unless we secure and protect it, it will erode; washed away in the rain, hidden behind the clutter, lost in the mess.

There are steps we can take to uncover and secure our dignity. The key is how we treat ourselves. We can begin to plant trees that will shade and nourish for years to come. We can cultivate the flowers and grasses that provide beauty and comfort. We can learn to restore the earth, to replace the lost nutrients and to give it rest when necessary. And as we begin to nurture and cherish our own dignity, others will come to respect it as well. Not only respect it, but enjoy it with us.

Dress With Dignity

☆ *A person of dignity dresses with dignity.* ☆

If we often dress sloppily we think poorly of ourselves. Some will say it works the other way—that people who think poorly of themselves dress sloppily. It works both ways. But we can easily control how we dress. I never cease to be amazed at the kind of clothes I allow myself to wear. I am constantly having to whip myself into doing better. It is only because I am trying to develop in myself a life-style of dignity that I have thrown away the underwear with stretched elastic that does stay up under panty hose, but not well. I forced myself to get rid of the drab housedresses that "do" around the house. *Panty hose that have tears and runs will be all right for wearing under slacks,* I used to tell myself. Poppycock! Am I not important enough to wear undies with good elastic and panty hose without runs? I certainly am! And I will! So I have thrown away the old "make do" stuff. Under the beautiful exterior I present, is respectable underwear. And it's not because I might get in an accident as my grandmother used to warn. I wear nice undies because *I* see and *I* care. A person of dignity wears nice underwear. It is a personal thing. *We do it for ourselves.*

Needless to say, the exterior follows the same trend. People who wish to upgrade their own self-esteem must make the effort to upgrade their outer appearance. Hair should not be neglected or droopy. Frequently, it is hard for Messies to realize the importance of this. We feel ideas and ideals are important. What we put on our bodies seems less important. Because we tend to neglect it, we must pay special attention to how we dress. It is the first step in our search for dignity. It will be the first clue to others that a change has begun in our lives.

> A person of worth wears clothes that are clean, neat, and in good repair. This means no stretched-out elastic, no panty hose with runs, no torn slips. She always maintains high personal standards, even on the things that don't show.

Speak With Dignity

☆ *A person of dignity speaks with dignity.* ☆

Recently I was at a small committee meeting. The chairman was a man of considerable dignity. He commanded the group basically by the way he spoke. Let me first of all say that he was British and had to his advantage an elegant British accent. That would not have been enough to command respect, however, if he had not used other techniques well. He spoke deliberately and somewhat more slowly than most. But perhaps most important, when he made points, he leaned forward slowly and looked directly into the eyes of those in the group. It was done ever so naturally, but it was commanding.

I would say that most of the people in the group spoke in a similar way. (The members of the group were mostly men who were in positions of leadership in their occupations.) When they spoke, they expected to be listened to, so they did not have to speak loudly or rapidly. In short, they spoke with confidence. What a contrast to many chatty, excited women's groups. Studies have shown that women are interrupted much more often than men. We feel we have to talk louder and faster to "get it in."

This matter of speaking with dignity has two sides. If we feel confident and in control, we will speak in a way that reflects it. It works the other way, too. If we speak confidently, deliberately, not in a high, fast voice, we will command respect from others. This will reinforce a sense of confident dignity in ourselves.

Agatha Christie, in one of her mysteries, describes just such a characteristic way of speaking. "Dr. Nicholson was a big man with a manner that suggested great reserves of power. His speech was slow, on the whole he said very little, but contrived somehow to make every word sound significant. He wore strong glasses and behind them his very blue eyes flittered reflectively." (*Why Didn't They Ask Evans?*)

People who respect themselves express their own feelings more often. They also speak more politely to other people because the people to whom they are speaking are considered valuable and important and should be treated with dignity. Instead of asking a favor ("Will you hand me the phone?"), confident people are much more likely to make a statement of their feelings ("I would like the phone, please," or, "I would appreciate it if you would hand me the phone"). It is the language of authority. It gets quicker action. Making statements about what you want carries much more weight than asking for what you want.

I saw an example of this at the committee meeting I mentioned earlier. At one point, when the work of the committee was slowed by unnecessary backtracking, the chairman leaned forward. In a quiet and open way he said, "I feel I must tell you that if we continue going over material we have already covered sufficiently, I shall become impatient." I was amazed to see the change. The backtracking stopped immediately.

Most of us would have said, "If we keep going back, the meeting will run late," or, "If we keep going back, we will confuse the issue." But he was a man of confidence. His feelings were in the best interest of the group. He spoke them freely.

Messies tend to be too friendly, too giving, and too open. Just as wearing sloppy clothes to save money is an unwise idea when carried too far, being too accommodating encourages people to treat us without respect. The way you talk can help correct this. Express your feelings clearly and unemotionally. You are a person of worth. Your thoughts and feelings count.

People of dignity speak of themselves in positive ways. Although they may be very open about their weaknesses, and we all have them, people of dignity do not speak of themselves in derogatory ways.

I am not encouraging a bragging attitude. Bragging is offensive. It is beneath a person of dignity. Perhaps it will be easy to see what I mean if you watch someone whom you really admire. See if they don't speak rather openly, *when appropriate,* about their strengths and successes. You should, too.

If you are an excellent seamstress and someone asks if you can sew, tell them. Say with a smile, "Yes, I am a very good seamstress," not, "I sew a little sometimes."

Finally, people will respect you if you have something valuable to say. Messies, being idea people, frequently are avid readers. We may read the morning newspaper, the *National Enquirer,* or *The Wall Street Journal*—but we generally do read. As a result, we are usually in tune with what is happening in the world. This will enable us to hold our own in most conversations. Keeping up with current interests will make us interesting people. That is certainly a plus. If you feel that you have let a little sluggishness of mind creep in and you need a jolt of enthusiasm or interest, why not consider going to college for a refresher course or taking a correspondence course? Studies have shown that people who have large vocabularies are more successful than those who have poor or mediocre vocabularies. You might enjoy getting a book on vocabulary improvement to rev up your word power. Have the cares of life pushed you away from the intellectual stimulation you really need to help your self-esteem and strengthen your concept of the importance of your own personal dignity? In your search for the dignity that may have slipped away, you must be sure not to neglect your own personal development.

A word of caution is needed, however. Don't sign up for anything that will take too much time and force you into that hurried and harried way of life that is robbing you of so much dignity already. Get things more under control before you begin any extensive commitment.

One more thing is necessary; being interesting is really not enough. Speaking in the proper tone or making the proper eye contact is not enough either. You must have something really worthwhile to say. People will *want* to hear what you have to say if it meets their needs—either their need to have certain information, their need to have the answer to a problem, or their need for understanding. Parroting clichés or talking in a surface way about unsolved problems will cause people to think less of you. They will know that you are not interacting with reality in a meaningful way. We need depth to our speech.

I am not suggesting that we attempt to change our personalities and become very stiff, looking over horn-rimmed glasses and issuing deep dictums. Many of us are bouncy, bubbly, and full of fun. Great! If that is you, be bouncy, bubbly, and full of fun. Perhaps you have a subtle but persistent sense of humor that pervades every aspect of your life. You can't keep it down. Wonderful! Hold on to that quality. I just want to remind you and myself that if we are interested in fun, humor, and friendliness only, we will lose that important aspect of our lives that makes us take ourselves seriously enough to care about the dignity we all enjoy. That will be reflected in our houses. People of dignity do not live in clutter. They live in order and beauty.

If you are depressed and your depression is affecting the house (or the house being so messy is affecting the depression), now is a good time to begin picking up one or two shreds of dignity at a time. Perhaps you can start to speak more confidently in your home or on the phone. Perhaps you will start stating your needs openly in a nonemotional way. Perhaps it will just be a new haircut or new underwear. Whatever it is it will be for you—because you are a person of worth.

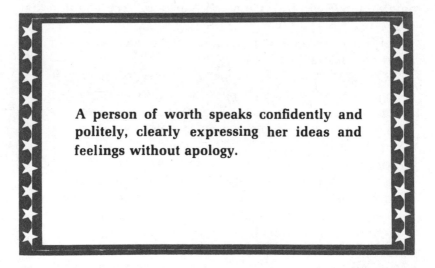

A person of worth speaks confidently and politely, clearly expressing her ideas and feelings without apology.

Act With Dignity

☆ **A person of dignity acts with dignity.** ☆

All of us have our doubts about our own personal value as people, if not at all times, at some times. It is at times like these that we need to remember some helpful things we can do to reinforce our own self-esteem.

It is always a good idea to seek out people who value you. Even if you are not going through a time of self-doubt, you need a friend, an acquaintance, or co-worker who thinks you are just great and knows how to tell you in a regular and responsible way. Family members play an important part here, but we may feel that they think we are great because they are prejudiced. I find that the more objective opinion of someone outside the family has a clearer ring of reality when the going is tough. Nothing, however, can take the place of constant reassurance and appreciation from family members on a day-to-day basis. Some people find that dogs or other pets who always love and admire them and think they are wonderful, give them a strong reinforcement of self-esteem.

Of course, the basis for it all is God's assessment of us. We *need* to know He thinks well of us. David was amazed at God's view of man and expressed it so beautifully in Psalms 8:3–5 (NAS) as he talked to God. "When I consider Thy heavens, the work of Thy fingers, the moon and the stars, which Thou hast ordained; What is man, that Thou dost take thought of him? And the son of man, that Thou dost care for him? Yet Thou hast made him a little lower than God, and dost crown him with glory and majesty!" The point is that people of dignity find ways to maintain the sense of worth they know is really theirs. (More will be said about this in chapter 9, "Rethink Your Position.")

A person of dignity acts like a person of dignity by refusing to let himself be put down by others. Just as he knows that putting down others is wrong because they are made in God's image and deserving of respect, so he does not allow it to be done to him. There are several ways to avoid being treated rudely or in a disrespectful way.

The first way is to just avoid people who do not have the good judgment to treat you properly. If there is someone who is "on your case," simply make it a point to see or speak to that person as little as possible. Don't avoid him or her because you are angry. Avoid them with the same sensible attitude that makes you avoid repeatedly putting your hand on a hot burner. It just does not make sense to continue an unsatisfactory action.

Many of us Messies, being open and friendly, find it hard to do this. As a moth is drawn to the flame, we come back again and again to the rude person because we think that surely we can get it straightened out. We think that if we are nice enough, friendly enough, clever enough with the retorts, or caustic enough with our answers, we can somehow change the person so that we will be treated properly by him. I have seldom found this to be the case. The person who has the poor judgment to treat me rudely in the first place, seldom has the good judgment to stop it.

Sometimes, because we work with certain people or because they are members of our families, we cannot avoid them completely. In that case, some other approach must be used to correct the situation. But correct it we must. We do not deserve to go on indefinitely being degraded by another person.

The first thing to do is to recognize that it is happening. Frequently, the put-down is subtle or disguised as humor. Face the fact that you are being put down and determine that it will not continue. After that it will not continue. Somehow, whether through humor, talking to the person in an unemotional but direct way, transferring elsewhere, speaking to the boss about the problem, or, in some cases, through a breakthrough in friendship (how about asking that person out to lunch?), we will make a change.

Let's back up a second and note specifically what we are not talking about. We are not talking about criticism. All of us do things that someone needs to tell us about. That's not disrespectful if it's done properly. We are not talking about a slipup of rudeness toward us. Everybody can make a mistake on a bad day. It's best to forgive and forget these things as quickly as possible.

We are not talking about everyday give and take which some of us who have sensitive spirits and low self-esteem may construe as rudeness. In that case, we should try to improve our own sense of self-worth and be a little more laid back in how we view our treatment. What we *are* talking about is a chronic, derogatory treatment, which is shown by the kind of criticism, the tone of criticism, the frequency of criticism, or derogatory humor.

I guess we all have had the misfortune to be involved in some of these situations. I recall once when the mother of one of my junior high students called me about a problem. As I talked to her, her attitude became belligerent; so I quietly said, "I'm afraid we are going to have to discontinue this conversation. I make it a policy not to talk to people who treat me in a disrespectful way. It would be better if you talked to the principal about this." She was flabbergasted. "You mean you won't talk to me!" I repeated my statement about my policy and I ended the conversation on a polite note. The problem was handled through the principal.

I follow this plan with my junior high students as well. On rare occasions students will be rude, sometimes without realizing it. If I talk in an explanatory way to them, letting them know that they are behaving in a way that, whether they mean it or not, is not respectful, they will usually change easily. (By the way, I always talk to them about their behavior in private because junior high students are very sensitive in front of their friends. I want to protect their dignity as well as my own.) If they continue to be rude, I immediately have someone else talk to them because, as you now know, I do not continue to talk to people who talk to me in a disrespectful way. Nor do I talk to others disrespectfully, at least I sure try not to. So far things have worked out well in these areas. In areas where I have less control over what goes on around me, things are not always so simple.

It may help to explain that I never ask for an apology from anyone who has been rude, whether child or adult. That is a personal decision on their part. I don't feel the need for one myself because I don't take rudeness as a personal affront so much as a failure of judgment on the other person's part.

Having said all this, let me hasten to mention that there are times when we bring trouble on ourselves. Not long ago, I was in the market for my first pair of glasses. It had been one of my New Year's goals, "Get an incredibly attractive pair of glasses." My sixteen-year-old son, a young lady friend from Trinidad, and I stopped in an eyeglass store in a mall. I tried one style and then another. Some looked funny. I put some on upside down. We got pretty silly. When I asked the man if he would open the case and show me a pair of glasses I had seen, he refused, saying that we were not seriously in the market for glasses. I felt he had been rude. He should have opened the case for us, I suppose; but looking back I can see that I brought it on myself. The man had no sense of humor. Perhaps he was tired. In actuality, I was an accomplice in his behavior.

Sometimes this happens to people on a much broader scale. Some people find that they get very little respect as a regular thing. Rodney Dangerfield has made a comedy career of it but when it happens in real life, it's not funny at all. If you find that from place to place with many different groups of people you are getting no respect, it is probably that you, like me in the eyeglass store, are cooperating. Most likely you do not know what brings on this treatment. Perhaps you think you know. "It's because I'm fat (or ugly or clumsy)," you may say. It is not any of these. One of the most respected men I know is a high school teacher with cerebral palsy. He speaks with a slur, cannot fully control the muscles of his face, and to top it all off sometimes comes to school wearing tennis shoes, army fatigue pants, a dress coat, and a tie. High school kids can be cannibals if they sense weakness of self-esteem. This man has not had any trouble. Someone has instilled in him a self-respect that has taken him many places more able-bodied people have not been able to go. It is not because of anything physical that we are treated badly. Physical problems sometimes become the focus of disrespect, but they are far from being the cause.

If you find that lack of respect follows you around like a cloud, try to find out why. Go to a counselor if you can find one who will work with you on social morés. Ask the counselor, "What can I do differently which will bring me the kind of acceptance that I deserve?" Pinpoint problems and work on them.

If you can't find outside help, try reading books on success. Begin to implement some of the techniques in this book. It is important for you to do this because you are a special person. There is nobody more deserving of the proper treatment than you.

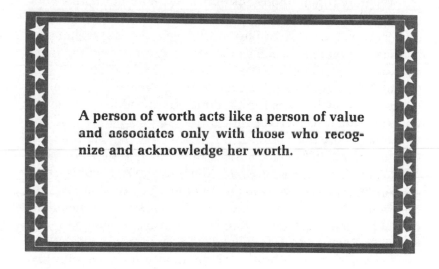

A person of worth acts like a person of value and associates only with those who recognize and acknowledge her worth.

React With Dignity

☆ *A person of worth (and we all are) reacts with dignity.* ☆

Messies tend to live in a particularly troubling world. On the one hand, we are aware of our own good capabilities, our strengths. On the other hand we find ourselves doing some very peculiar things which make us feel as though any confidence in our own worth is misplaced. The characteristics that make housekeeping difficult for us, also make us relate to other areas of life uncertainly.

We may forget important things, we may not notice obvious items, or we may mistake simple facts. We may try to overcome our weaknesses by using organizational techniques. We can use planning such as the Mount Vernon method to get the house under control. We can use the M.A. Flipper System (see chapter 12) to keep it under control. We can use other organizational techniques for handling our schedules and activities. But there are certain things that cannot be planned for. Once I wore my pull-on slacks to school backwards. I thought I was losing weight when I noticed how baggy they were in the front. Two hours later I discovered my mistake. There is no organizational plan for how to put on pants. You don't make a list that says, "Put pants on frontways." There is no organizational plan that keeps me from letting my bathtub overflow because I forgot it. Everybody makes a mistake once in a while. When this becomes a way of life, as is commonly the case with harried Messies, it can get very discouraging. It eats away at self-esteem.

If we do klutzy things in front of others, we feel even more like dunces than ever. How we react *after* we've done these things is very important. Let's look at some mental approaches we can prepare ahead of time.

We have already talked about avoiding those who put us down regularly. When we do something particularly dumb in front of others, we must be prepared to handle it. Even people who are usually nice may be tempted to make a hurtful or funny crack. Don't let it throw you. Accept yourself and it will be easier. If you wear your pants backwards and someone mentions that this is the situation, tell them that you are a trend setter. If the tub overflows, tell them that you are doing a really great cleaning job on the bathroom floor—and the hall floor, and the bedroom floor.... It *is* upsetting to do these things. We would much rather be like those in-control people who have never done anything awkward as far as anyone can tell. Messies work with a high degree of error. The point is that we must work harder to overcome our upset as quickly as possible. As our self-esteem grows, the time between our misstep and our forgiveness of ourselves will shorten. We will be able to accept ourselves for what we are, warts and all, and enjoy those aspects of our lives that are more successful.

When awkward things happen, avoid the tendency to make excuses. As I was outlining this chapter one Wednesday morning, happily anticipating my final day of vacation before returning to school, I suddenly realized that WEDNESDAY *was* the day I was supposed to return to school. The faculty meeting was scheduled for 8:30 A.M. and it was already 8:45. My first impulse was to berate myself for my oversight while frantically scurrying around, then race to the meeting. Once there, I could mutter my flustered excuses. But I remembered my own advice. I am a person of dignity and worth. No dumb thing I can do can alter that fact. I had been looking forward to making a nice appearance at school on my first day. I had recently had my hair done in anticipation of school beginning. I wanted to fix it right. So I forgave myself, got dressed carefully, did my hair and makeup, and drove carefully to school, enjoying the beauty of the morning. I arrived unusually happy and joined the meeting which, as it happens, had begun late. I was just in time to introduce myself as though I had been there all along. No one asked me why I was late, if they noticed at all. Several people did tell me how nice I looked.

I am a person crowned with glory and majesty by God even when I am late to the school meeting, forget my bathtub, wear my pants backwards, or do any of the thousands of other things I am likely to do which are not so easily solved.

But what happens when we get really down and very discouraged with ourselves and things begin to unravel? What happens when our faults catch up with us and we are overwhelmed by self-doubt?

The best thing to do is to remember the successes. There are certain things about myself I am proud of. You have some, too. Tell yourself, *I know I goofed up here but I* _____ (fill in the good stuff here). Everybody should have something to remember in more rational moments.

But sometimes no amount of talking to ourselves can convince us that we have *any* good qualities. We are depressed. We do not deserve to feel like that. Outside help from a psychologist may be needed.

You are valuable, not because you think so or because others think so but because God thinks so. Even if you are so depressed you don't ever get out of bed and you never pick up even one piece of clutter, you are infinitely important. You don't even have to believe it one little bit for it to be true. Just count on it—you are marvelously, wonderfully valuable. Period!

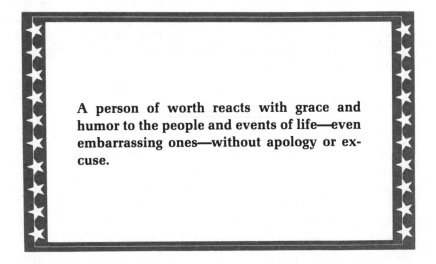

A person of worth reacts with grace and humor to the people and events of life—even embarrassing ones—without apology or excuse.

Treat Yourself With Dignity

☆ *A person of dignity treats herself with dignity.* ☆

The basis of being a person of dignity is our own self-respect. When we respect ourselves, others will respect us. We must think of ourselves as people of great value. It will make a big difference in every aspect of our lives, including our houses. Our houses reflect our own personal attitudes about ourselves.

You will notice I have shared a number of things about myself which some people might wish to hide. I freely share that I work with a high degree of error because my own worth does not rise and fall in relation to how many dumb things I can cover up. I am made in God's image. I am important to Him. I am one of that special group of people known as *Humanus Wonderfulus* subspecies Messie.

This is precisely the reason that we don't make excuses. We do not need to hedge in our nobility by pretended perfection. It exists perfectly well without our paltry efforts to protect it.

Excuse me while I adjust my crown.

BADARACLO

49

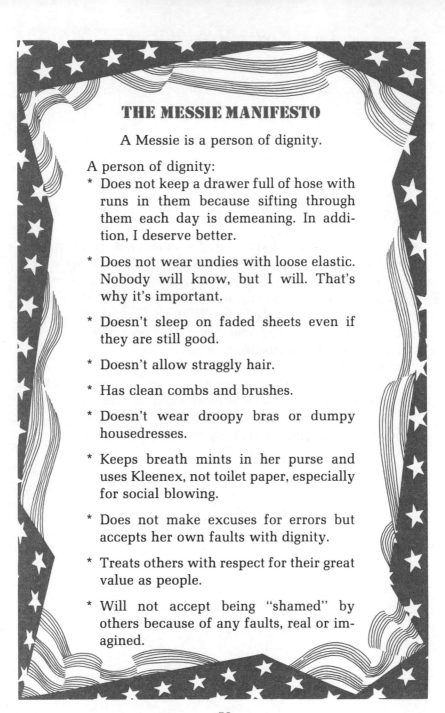

THE MESSIE MANIFESTO

A Messie is a person of dignity.

A person of dignity:

* Does not keep a drawer full of hose with runs in them because sifting through them each day is demeaning. In addition, I deserve better.

* Does not wear undies with loose elastic. Nobody will know, but I will. That's why it's important.

* Doesn't sleep on faded sheets even if they are still good.

* Doesn't allow straggly hair.

* Has clean combs and brushes.

* Doesn't wear droopy bras or dumpy housedresses.

* Keeps breath mints in her purse and uses Kleenex, not toilet paper, especially for social blowing.

* Does not make excuses for errors but accepts her own faults with dignity.

* Treats others with respect for their great value as people.

* Will not accept being "shamed" by others because of any faults, real or imagined.

"We know what a man thinks not when he tells us what he thinks, but by his actions."

ISAAC BASHEVIS SINGER

Messiness is, for the most part, something we are born with. I have been a Messie all my life, but I didn't know it until I tried to organize my house for myself. Until that time, I had lived in the organization that my mother, the Cleanie, produced. When I had trouble with organization, she always kept me steered in the right direction and floated me along when I floundered organizationally. All of this help I took as a matter of course and didn't realize how messy I was when I was on my own.

Lurking in my brain was a closet full of destructive thinking and a trunk full of characteristics that would later sink my organizational ship. Right from the beginning of my marriage, when I started housekeeping on my own, I started in the wrong direction.

Many Messies share characteristics that make it hard for us to succeed in housekeeping. Let's look at some of these characteristics Messies have in common.

Distractibility

Like a flea in a frying pan, Messies hop from one task to another, leaving a trail of half-done tasks behind them. Without actually deciding to leave one job, they find themselves another. The cluttered nature of the house invites this. We hop from one job to another because in order to put away things from one pile, we must clear a shelf to receive the overflow from another shelf, and so on.

Finally, husband comes home and it is left for tomorrow—or whenever we can get back to it.

The Flipper system, which is described in chapter 12, is designed to give direction and purpose to our labor so we won't squander our energy on playing musical messes.

Visual Tune Out

Messies don't really "notice" how bad things are because they don't actually focus on things visually. You might say they *think* nearsighted. They may have good visual acuity, but they don't "look" at the condition of the house. Messies have a sort of tunnel vision. They can see only a little part of the house at a time, working like crazy on that. This accounts for one part of the house being in super shape while the rest is a shambles.

Tendency to Overdo

Because they really do want to succeed in the house and know they are distractible, Messies frequently get so tense that they overdo. They are so intense that they keep on too long. If Messies could relax and stand back from the whole issue of housekeeping, they could make a lot more progress.

This overdoing can show itself in several ways. Peg, for instance, wants desperately to have a nice orderly home so she begins with the drawers of the dresser. All day she sorts socks, folds clothes, lines drawers, and so on. Meals are left uncooked and laundry is left undone. So anxious is she to succeed and so strong is her concentration that she becomes rigid. She cannot shift into other jobs when they need doing. The house is too disordered to clean. But the drawers are neat.

Mattie has a different problem but the result is the same. Mattie is able to see the bigger picture. Her goal is to do the whole house—to get control once and for all. It must be done. She is determined. Hour after hour she labors, doing a Herculean task spurred on by desperation. She cannot slow down because her concentration on success is so strong. If the children interrupt, as they always do, she cannot handle the shift she must make for the interruption. She may become angry at them and quit the job altogether. She cannot shift from the house to the kids and back to the house.

Peg becomes discouraged because the really troublesome parts of the house are not done and Mattie becomes exhausted. They both quit for a long rest. Again, they overdo. This time they overdo resting. The house gathers dust while they read (or whatever) to escape the burden of overdoing.

Now they have a really good excuse to tell themselves: *I tried but it was just too much for me.*

The Mount Vernon method is designed to keep a person from getting on the wrong unproductive track like Peg or on the overdoing track like Mattie, while getting the house under control. "Inch by inch it's a cinch" is our motto. But the inches must be directed in the right direction or we quit.

Slow Movements

Some Messies move slower than other people. Our Dan Marino, super Miami Dolphins quarterback, has what physical therapists call a "fast twitch." His synapses and nerves just work quickly. He'll be standing in the pocket under pressure and all of a sudden the ball is gone. He moves like lightning. He was born with a fast twitch.

Many Messies have slow twitches. We seem to be working at the same rate as others but less gets done. Those who do have fast twitches sometimes use it as an excuse to procrastinate because they will get it done quickly once they begin. But they put off beginning.

These and other similar characteristics actually interfere with housekeeping successes. Cleanies aren't troubled with these hindrances.

Messies Anonymous assumes that anybody who is a Messie wouldn't be that way if it were a matter of choice. But we were born with these characteristics, just as we were born with our hair and eye color. There are other hindrances we bring on ourselves. These are ways of thinking we pick up along the way to help us adjust to our messy way of life. In the end, these "adjustments" add to the problem.

Many Messies are just "laid back" types. That's why we need a specific, easy-to-follow plan, designed to fit personal characteristics. Perhaps some of us had the spirit of the 1960s. We persuaded ourselves that it was not necessary to be too intense about life. We were already disorganized by nature, and the undisciplined life-style was in vogue. This combination moves a Messie a long way down the road to disastrous housekeeping.

To add to our problems, Messies are able to absorb vast quantities of personal stress. We are used to having things out of control. We can take it. We know we won't die if the phone is disconnected (they can reconnect it), if a check bounces (they'll put it through again), if there's no food for breakfast (we'll have SpaghettiOs), if a report is not ready (nobody's perfect), if we can't find the tax receipts (it's only money). This kind of living is devastating to a person's self-esteem. Because we can handle it, we let it continue, not realizing how devastating it really is to us. Messies cannot allow their dignity to be trampled on. We should not allow ourselves to "take it."

A banker I know told me that he had customers who knew they were overdrawn and who had the money to deposit but just did not bother to come to the bank to make the deposit. "Lazy," he called them. But I wonder. Why would a person be willing to take the consequence rather than put forth a little effort to avoid it?

Perhaps one reason is that same rebellious nature that causes some people to procrastinate. *You aren't going to tell me what I have to do,* they think consciously or unconsciously, and so they break the rules and take the consequences.

Finally, Messies kid themselves by hanging on to unproductive ideas. The energy-saving idea of leaving things out so the items don't need to be taken out again just makes a mess. But the idea *sounds* good. The idea of piling, not filing, doesn't work either, but it seems like such a time-saver. The fruitless idea of having six boxes of Band-Aids around somewhere so when I need them surely I'll be able to find one, doesn't work either. These ideas make for a messy way of life. They must be abandoned if a new way of life is to emerge.

While the Messie is struggling to overcome her natural characteristics and her unproductive ways of thinking, other people are entering into the picture. Husbands, children, and parents who are disturbed by having to live in this commotion eventually begin to state their feelings about the way things are.

"You need to put things away so I can find them."
"Why don't you keep the house looking like Carrie's mommy does?"
"I don't have any clean underwear to wear today."

We can react in several ways to their chiding. We can—

Rebel. I have already referred to those Messies who react in a rebellious way, become angry, and don't change—just for spite.

Retreat. Some Messies react by withdrawing. They get too upset to do anything. Sometimes they become depressed and spend long hours in bed or reading or just doing a few things they are successful at and ignoring the rest.

Use smoke screens. This is a Messie who may seem always to be working or about to work or talking about work or planning to work, but she never gets much done. She may really be trying, but not to accomplish what her family wants—a beautiful house. She uses talk to cover her lack of actual accomplishment. When she does work it is not to accomplish the job, it is simply to say she's done it. This Messie is not goal oriented, she is task oriented. She does not pick up the house because she wants it to look beautiful and work efficiently. She cleans because that's what is expected of her; that's what she's *supposed* to do. She may vacuum at the end of the day because it's on her list. A Cleanie would vacuum in the morning because she wants a lovely home all day.

Messies play all kinds of games with themselves but they always come up losers. When Messies realize they have some characteristics that make organization difficult, they can compensate for them. Accepting ourselves with our weaknesses will help relax us and free us to work more efficiently. When we realize there are ways of thinking we need to abandon, success is just a thought away.

CHAPTER

6

Profile of a Messie (Part II): The Personalities

"Imitations abound but there's only one YOU."
FLORENCE LITTAUER (*Personality Plus*)

Twenty-five years ago I was introduced to the four basic temperaments originally propounded by Hippocrates, the Greek physician who is generally credited with being the father of modern medicine. All through the years, people have tried to divide humans into some type of meaningful classification. Although no system really divides people with perfect accuracy, this ancient Greek classification certainly can give us some significant insights into ourselves and those we live with—and try to understand. The names for these temperaments may sound Greek to you, but we will stick with them so as not to buck twenty-five hundred years of history.

Here are the four types with their basic personality traits:

Sanguine—Lively, sunny outlook
Melancholy—Dark, moody outlook
Choleric—Active
Phlegmatic—Slow temperament

No person is purely one temperament. We are all combinations. Most people, however, have one dominant personality type. Understand your basic type and the types of the people you live with and you will understand some of the problems you have been having with yourself and with them. Since it is true that opposites attract, this is important!

Characteristics of the Personality Types—
Which Type Are You?

Sanguine. Sanguine types are outgoing, lively, and exuberant. Generally optimistic and not easily bored, they have many interests to which they can turn and are frequently involved in crafts, art, and volunteer work.

Sanguines tend to have spotty memories. Things like names, dates, and places tend to fade rapidly.

Because Sanguines live in the present, the past fades rapidly from memory and they are unable to visualize the future with any clarity. I believe this is the reason so many Sanguine Messies collect things. They know, intuitively, that the past will fade and they will not be able to remember it. In order to compensate, they make a Herculean effort to insure that it doesn't slip. They take and keep gigantic amounts of snapshots. They keep old programs, canceled ticket stubs, shells from the beach, and baby shoes. They have good reason to: Without them, they probably won't remember the past with the richness they feel it deserves. Being responsible people, Sanguines want to be prepared for the future. Since they cannot visualize the future well (and who can know exactly the future?), they go overboard on being prepared. They keep old medicine, magazines, and makeup "just in case." The problem with this is that unless they are highly organized, they can't enjoy or even *find* all these items they have collected. Even the organized Sanguine finds that all of this organized "collection" becomes too much burden to bear.

This living in the present with little regard to the future is also a problem when it comes to keeping a time schedule. Even though Sanguines may know they have to be someplace at a certain time, they find it difficult to pace themselves to get dressed and drive there in the proper amount of time. When it comes to remembering things to do in the future, Sanguines are very unreliable, often forgetting events or getting the time or day mixed up. Because I am a Sanguine, as are many Messies, I missed the opening day of school, as I mentioned earlier. This is also one of the reasons bills are allowed to become overdue. The time passes quickly before the Sanguine realizes that the date for sending the payment has passed. It seems as if the bill just came a few days before.

Because Sanguines live in the present, they have difficulty with long-range goals. Although they may take on several projects and volunteer for many worthy activities, they have a problem following through. The goal begins to fade quickly. Other, "fresher" activities catch their attention. The goal that was so important yesterday, drifts into the murky past.

Many Messies have the basic Sanguine nature. If they live with another Sanguine, there is double trouble for the house. They will be cheerful but always frustrated with the state of things in the world around them.

Melancholy. Melancholies have a very rich temperament. They are very sensitive, which means they usually enjoy the fine arts. Indeed, they may be musicians, artists, inventors, philosophers, or theologians.

Melancholies are sensitive to the needs of others. They do not forget them like the Sanguine does. They remember and analyze the needs of the person, because they love to meet needs whether personal or of some other nature. They are idealistic, purposeful, and organized.

Most Melancholies are perfectionists. They love to analyze things to see how close to perfection they come. They also love details and are very visually sensitive. Melancholies love to make charts, graphs, and lists. They live best in a house that is orderly and serene. Because of these characteristics, they make good housekeepers—evaluating what needs to be done and doing it efficiently. They are economical, as well. If you are part Melancholy, you can use this artistic and sensitive characteristic to encourage yourself to keep going. Go to model homes and displays of beauty. Dream of the beauty and order that will be yours if you keep going with your plans. You can make your home your art.

If you live with a full Melancholy, he or she is probably grieved at your messy tendencies. The disorder and lack of perfection drives them crazy. Nothing a Messie does is ever good enough for a Melancholy. He will redo it or be forced to say something about it, blurting out hurtful things. He may even exaggerate some problems, making you feel further confused and frustrated.

If you are a Sanguine personality, all of this perfection and depression from the Melancholy you live with can drive you crazy and eventually discourage you from trying. If you are a Messie with some Melancholy tendencies, these traits can cause you to procrastinate or put yourself down because you take so seriously your own faults.

Choleric. Cholerics have optimistic, take-charge, goal-oriented, dynamic personalities. They are always trying to change things for the better and are frequently put in positions of leadership for that purpose. What's more, they know how to organize and delegate work.

Does this sound like a person who would be controlled by a messy house? Not on your life! If you are a Messie who has even a touch of Choleric, use it. Nurture it and use it. It will help you immensely to get on the right track.

If your husband or mother or mother-in-law is a Choleric, you may find yourself being highly pressured and criticized. Because they are goal-oriented, they sometimes (perhaps frequently) ignore the feelings of the people they relate to. They look down on people less capable than themselves.

If you live with a Choleric who has not learned to tone down his pushy nature when dealing with you, you may find your relationship strained by this bossy approach. This may discourage or anger you to the point that you do an even poorer job of keeping house than you would have otherwise.

Cholerics are hard to change. If a Choleric is interfering with your life by his abrasive approach, you need to let him know that. He is sure he is right and that if you would only change, he would not have to push you. However, clear communication, oiled by love and caring, should begin to make a change. A person of dignity, Messie or not, doesn't allow herself to be chronically put down, no matter how capable the one who puts us down is.

On the other hand, Messies can use the organizational abilities of Cholerics once the tension between them is dispelled. The Choleric can help guide a Messie to success, if the Messie is the one who initially asks for advice. Thank God for Cholerics. They are the movers and shakers of the world. Let's get them to help us, not boss us.

Phlegmatic. Phlegmatics are easygoing people. Many Messies have a large touch of Phlegmatic. They are steady, low-keyed, patient, and accommodating. Phlegmatics are good workers in any organization. They may not set the world on fire with enthusiasm or creativity, but they can be counted on to get the job done.

Most Phlegmatics are happily reconciled to life and are not pushy. Although they do not take control of situations automatically as do Cholerics, if put in a position of responsibility they feel they can handle, they will usually do a very good job.

Phlegmatics are good listeners. They are not restless to get on to other things as Sanguines are. They make good, easy-to-get-along-with friends and are always there when you need them.

Phlegmatics may have fewer weaknesses than other types, but the weaknesses they do have are significant to Messies with Phlegmatic tendencies.

Phlegmatics are not easily motivated and do not have much get-up-and-go. They prefer not to make plans to do things such as go out to a play, remodel the house, or upgrade housekeeping. It's easier not to. The saying, "Let's not and say we did," fits the Phlegmatic. In its most extreme form, this low motivation is called laziness.

Phlegmatics prefer to *think* about things to do rather than *do* them. The fact that they have thought out a job carefully often substitutes for actually doing it. Mentally, they are very efficient, always thinking of how to save energy by doing things in an easier way. They feel content knowing they are all prepared mentally to do the job if they ever get around to it—but they usually don't get around to it.

When it comes to housecleaning, the big job which would be necessary to get things in order just overwhelms them. They have a low-energy level. They may go to a seminar or read a book and be content with knowing *how* to change even if they never do.

This is low motivation further compounded by the Phlegmatic's tendency to be stubborn. If a Phlegmatic decides not to change, even a Choleric cannot persuade her to do so. The low motivation is "set" by stubbornness. An easygoing good humor often disguises this trait—but it is there.

Finally, Phlegmatics tend to be indecisive. Melancholies are indecisive because they want to make only the "best" decision in their perfectionistic way. Phlegmatics, however, hesitate to make decisions for more practical reasons. First of all, they are so easygoing, they don't really care about some choices. "Coffee or tea," "milk or Coke"—what difference does it make? None, to Phlegmatics. They let others order first and get what the majority wants.

The other reason Phlegmatics hesitate to make decisions is because they are protective of their energies and commitments. They do not want to make a decision that will later require them to do more work than they really want to do.

If a Messie woman lives with a Messie Phlegmatic man, she may have a tough time getting him to cooperate in her desire to change the house. After she gets the house in order and is wonderfully proud, he will not compliment her because he really doesn't care whether it is neat or not. Don't let this discourage you. It is his nature. Besides, you care even if he doesn't.

The Messie Temperament. Perhaps there is a fifth temperament which combines the temperaments of the other four groups in such a way as to make it a separate temperament—the Messie temperament.

Messies are frequently confused and frustrated by their own temperament. It contains a combination of conflicting characteristics of the other groups in varying combinations.

Messies have the friendliness, poor memory, cheery disposition, distractibility, and reluctance to say no of the Sanguine. Most Messies are basically Sanguine.

You can take advantage of this part of yourself. Use your friendliness and cheerfulness to encourage yourself to clean up the house. Invite people over, schedule get-togethers. This is a perfect reason for the Sanguine Messie to get the house in order.

Messies also have the Melancholy's sensitivity and desire for true values of life such as art, beauty, and learning, which causes great stress to their soul. So they compensate by using their natural ability to not notice the mess. To complicate things further, Messies are frequently perfectionists like Melancholies. This perfectionism along with the habit of collecting are the major impediments to progress. Perfectionism is a most frustrating characteristic because it works against itself. It has the seeds of destruction built in. As you know, the perfectionist Messies want to do it right or not at all and, too often, "not at all" wins. However, the Melancholy part can be one of the Messie's strongest motivations. Because this part makes them desire a quality way of life, they are often able to overcome hindrances and keep going over the problems until success is achieved.

The Phlegmatic part of the Messie that can be the most troublesome is low motivation—the feeling that everything is "just too much." The Messie with this trait needs to set up a reasonable program for herself. She should do a little Mount Vernoning every day. And when she sets up her Flipper, she has to make sure she doesn't overschedule and thereby discourage herself because it is too much.

Use Your Knowledge

Knowing about these temperaments can help you see yourself with all your strengths and weaknesses. You can then encourage your strengths and work either over or around your weaknesses. Weaknesses are never excuses for failure. They are only hindrances to avoid as you aim for success. Remember, whatever your temperament, you will succeed if you have a goal, have a keen desire to achieve it, and have a plan to do so.

If some of the characteristics you see here are those of the people you live with, learn to use and draw upon the positive characteristics and to overcome the negative ones.

Winning the War and Keeping It Won

PART TWO

CHAPTER

7

Victor or Victim: It's Really Up to You

Habit is habit, and not to be flung out the window by any man but coaxed downstairs a step at a time.

MARK TWAIN

Somewhere, hidden away, is our desire to improve our way of life. We must find it and nurture it. We must come to the realization that we and we alone are responsible for the condition in which we live. This understanding may come slowly or with the shock of a glass of cold water in the face. But it must come. The impact of this realization will result in a delightful life change you have been afraid to dream of.

We must realize that the house, with all its clutter and disorder, is the direct and deliberate creation of our own desires. The decisions we have made created it. We may not like what we have created—but create it we did! And only we can "uncreate" it.

Mother is not going to make the change for us. No fairy godmother is going to do it. No psychologist is going to come with his truck and haul stuff away. Neighbors or the health department are not ultimately responsible. We are.

True dignity begins when we plant our feet squarely in the middle of our lives and say, "I am responsible."

What a burden it lifts from our backs. No longer do we have to search for some cure, hoping and wondering from whence it may come charging up on a white horse, with some magic formula for success. *We are the cure.*

There is no secret of success written on a green stick hidden in the forest as Dostoevski thought as a child.

Once upon a time there was a man whose chief goal in life was to make his fortune by finding diamonds. He left his village to search the world over for these diamonds. He spent his life in this fruitless search and died a poor man. When his friends in the village dug his grave, they dug up incredibly valuable and beautiful *diamonds!* He had been searching in the wrong place. What he wanted had been close at hand all the time. Yet he died unfulfilled.

The answer you seek is close at hand. It is within you. If you keep searching in other places, you will waste time and miss out on the incredibly beautiful and wonderful life that is available for you. Grab it! Insist on it! But first admit, "The answer is within *me.*"

It is not easy to admit this. We have been telling ourselves for so long that we must save unnecessary items, that we must keep busy, that we deserve to rest, that we must follow the self-destructive path we have been following. It is hard to admit to ourselves that we have been wrong. We've been feeding ourselves destructive thoughts. It takes courage to say, "I have been wrong." Find that courage! You must—if you are ever going to find the answer to your dilemma.

Life often works on paradoxes. We have sayings to show that. We say that we "get by giving," we say, "more is less," and so on. In the area which we are talking about there is a similar principle—we improve by not trying so hard. Messies are rather intense people. Our intensity drives us to a frenzied life of saving, studying, doing, and going. To us everything is *so* important. We *must* keep this. We *must* do that. This way of thinking leads to cluttered lives and cluttered minds.

Just *relax!* Every detail of your life is not all that important. So you threw away a pan yesterday that you hadn't used in years but could use today. Who cares? You have another one that will do. Things don't have to be as elaborate and perfect as you've been telling yourself they need to be.

You are not the only person who can direct the school carnival which saps your life every year. Relax, let somebody else do it. Even if it is not done as well as you would have done it, who cares? It really is not all that important that every detail be done exactly as you would have done it. Even if (horror of horrors!) the school carnival isn't held unless you head it up, so what? Is there that little interest on the part of all of the other parents? The history of the world will not be changed if the school carnival is not held.

"Oh, but I love to do it," you say. "The children have so much fun!" But how about *your* children when they come home? Is it fun to have clutter all around or no clean socks when the morning rush comes?

We cannot have everything, and, what's more, it is not important that we do. Wake up to that fact and you will find the freedom to begin having the great life you want. You don't need to do everything. You don't need to *keep* everything. You don't need to read the newspaper through each day *and* do the crossword puzzle. "Thou shalt read every newspaper religiously," is not the eleventh commandment. After a while all the clutter and activity we gather to ourselves confuses us so much we don't even know what we need or want. We are just on a treadmill of bad habits.

Stop! Deliberately step off that treadmill. Decide now that you will *not* continue the way you have been going.

Somewhere in the past you decided, decision by decision, to get on the treadmill. Today, you can make a decision again—the decision to get off. Choose what you want now.

Perhaps you are afraid to get off—to let go of the way of life that you have told yourself makes you valuable and fulfilled. Perhaps you are afraid you will lose part of yourself. On the contrary, only as you take control will you be able to find your true self.

If you will not get off you have become a victim of your thoughts. Nobody knows the fear that comes to the heart of a Messie who must make that decision. We have become so attached to our destructive ways. I know there are Messies reading this right now who are afraid to think about letting go of these destructive patterns. The change may come with regrets—it may come with tears, first tears of loss and then tears of relief. You may valiantly start to let go and later turn back. That's okay as long as you know that when you have gotten the courage again, you will return to the new way of life you have chosen.

Challenge your fears. Tell yourself out loud and in writing that your life will be better when you quit striving so hard. Tell yourself that it will be okay for you to relax and not work so intensely on every detail. Tell yourself you will not lose part of yourself. You will gain the dignity and self-esteem you lost in the scramble of that other way of life.

There are two different approaches that readers who want to change will take.

Some who read this chapter will be infused with a fighting spirit. "How dare this house do this to my life!" they'll say as they get angry and roll up their sleeves to begin the fray. This attitude is very important. When we get angry, we will fight to make a change.

In California, a serial rapist had accosted and raped many women and no one seemed to be able to stop him. One young lady was jogging in the daylight hours when this same rapist jumped her from behind, knocking her to the ground and falling on top of her. He was much heavier and stronger than she but she was infused with anger and indignation. She would *not* be a victim. In her determination, she did her best to fight. All she could do was hit him in the throat with one free hand, but she did it so convincingly that he gave up and presumably went in search of an easier victim. The women who told this story were running a program on self-defense. They told how some of the women they talked to were reluctant to fight. Women attending the class said that they would fight to protect their children but would hesitate to fight to protect themselves. Our children are important, but we are important, too. Their statement was that self-respect is the basis of self-defense. Self-respect is the basis of our self-defense against messiness, too. When we respect ourselves, we will fight and win.

There is another helpful attitude which is good to adopt. In the long run, this attitude is probably one that will sustain the Messie over a longer period of time than anger because anger is hard to sustain. Sometimes in a flash of insight, the Messie will see the ridiculous nature of her situation. On a cloud of self-respect, like having an out-of-body experience, she rises above the house and looks down. She feels powerful. She laughs at how foolish she has been to have been dominated and defeated by the house. She will not fight the house. *We only fight with equals,* she reasons. She will not give the problem the courtesy of being considered an equal. The problem is large but she sees suddenly that her ability is so much larger. Almost regally, she begins banishing the problem. She doesn't fight it away. She simply dismisses it a little at a time. Slowly but surely it disappears because of the force of her mind. She has changed her thinking about herself and her house. In a sense, she loves the house into order. This attitude is a powerful force. The mess, no matter how big, cannot resist its power. This book may be the thing that opens your eyes to your own power.

A wonderful way of life awaits you. You can have the life you want. The secret really is within you.

Six Strategic Steps

The desire to change carries within it the seeds of its own fulfillment.

NAPOLEON HILL

Those Cleanies on the opposite end of the continuum from Messies are remarkable people. As I circulate across the country representing Messies Anonymous, I meet many different kinds of people, including that remarkable group known as Cleanies.

Cleanies hearing about Messies Anonymous feel this is an opportunity to tell me about the condition of their houses. They feel compelled to talk about it.

"My house is always perfect," the older professional man was telling me with his Spanish accent from behind his big desk. I had come to see him for business reasons but he had digressed to a subject he cared greatly about.

"I do not expect anybody to come visit me but if you were to come home with me right now, my house would look like a picture in a magazine. And I throw things out—always throw things out. I cannot stand things out of order. I don't know why. It is a sickness with me."

So went the conversation. It was like many other conversations I've had with Cleanies who love to talk about their beautiful houses. With Cleanies, the order of the house at this moment—right now—is a big thing.

What makes Cleanies different from Messies? When you really understand this basic difference you will know the secret of success. The thing that makes Cleanies so successful in controlling their houses is *desire*—a strong, burning, consistent, heartfelt desire to have a beautiful home at all times.

You already have some of that desire since you are reading this book. If you can make it intense enough, it will be the force behind your changing. We are not talking about a general wish or a vague hope. When you can see the house in your mind, when you can feel the joy you'll have when it's that way, when you cannot imagine things continuing the way they are now— then you have the desire you need for success.

In 1937, Napoleon Hill wrote a gentle, insightful book with the startling title *Think and Grow Rich*. This book, reprinted many times and still going strong, was probably the first book to expound the power of thought to accomplish what you want, provided you know what you want—and we know that, don't we! We want lovely, orderly houses! That's it, Mr. Hill! Mr. Hill should have written a book entitled *Think and Grow Neat*. The power of thought works for any goal, provided you know what you want and have the desire to accomplish it.

There are six steps to accomplishing what you want. These have been adapted many times to various goals. We will apply them to having a beautiful house because that's what we want.

1. *Decide exactly what you want.* Don't say, "I want a generally nice house." Decide *exactly* what you want. Make it definite. Do you want it nice in the public areas at all times so guests can always be welcomed, even unexpectedly? Or do you want it beautiful so you can enjoy being at home and seeing it? Or do you want it to be uncluttered so that the house can reflect your own personality? Or do you just want to quit losing things? Perhaps it is all of the above. Whatever *you* want. De-

cide now. Stop a minute to pinpoint your desire. Say it out loud to yourself before reading on.

2. *Decide what you will do to get it.* "There's no such thing as a free lunch." Keeping the house orderly is going to cost you; but living with it the way it is now is costing you already. The price you pay in lost time, lost self-esteem, lost money because of waste, misplaced papers, and so on is enormous. Decide what you are willing to give (or give up) in order to get what you want. That is your payment for a lovely home.

3. *Set a time limit.* Put a date on *when* your goal will be accomplished. Stop a moment and fix a definite time. Be realistic. It took me three and a half months to do the Mount Vernon method to my house and it is not large. After the Mount Vernon method, the Flipper System takes over (more about that later). Announce your target date out loud.

4. *Make a plan.* Decide on exactly *how* you will accomplish your goal. The Mount Vernon method, including a few daily jobs, is the way to start. Begin right away, whether you think you are ready or not. Include any other steps necessary to your plan.

5. *Make the above steps definite by writing them down.* Get a piece of paper and pen. Write exactly how you want your house to be and tell what you'll do to get it that way. Put down a time limit. Put that piece of paper in this book right now so you won't have it just floating around the house. If you want to put it on the refrigerator or bulletin board, that's okay, but have a definite place and keep it there.

6. *Read aloud the statement you have just written twice a day.* Read it when you get up in the morning and when you go to bed. Form a mental picture of your lovely house as you read. Feel the elation as though your house is already exactly as you want it.

Now you are mentally ready to begin. Success comes to those who are ready for it.

Strange as it may seem, your past failures may be just the trigger you need to flip you into success. If things had not gotten as bad as they are, you wouldn't be as willing to change as you are.

In my case, though, I had lived for twenty-three years in a chronically frustrating state of messiness that was growing very tiresome, indeed. It was a leak in the sink that finally made me change. I had kept stacks of newspapers under my sink because I might need them "just in case." The sink sprang a slow leak, but, because the newspapers soaked up the water, I didn't know about the leak until the floor of the cabinet had rotted. This was the final indignity. I suddenly saw the state to which my faulty thinking had reduced me. I was angry at what I had done to myself. It was the beginning of the end of my chronically Messie way of life. I didn't know how, but I knew I would change.

How much I have changed was pinpointed this morning as I made plans for the day with my husband.

"I'm going to the university library to write for a few hours," I said.

"You can't," he answered in a surprised voice. "My mother is coming for an overnight visit. Don't you need to clean house?"

"What needs cleaning?" I asked. "The bed is made. The dishes are in the dishwasher washing. The rug was just vacuumed and the furniture polished. There's nothing to do."

"You could do the toilet, the tub, the bathroom sink."

"We don't have a bathroom sink," I reminded him. (We had had it replaced but the replacement was faulty, so we were "between sinks." It certainly cuts down on cleaning the bathroom.)

"Well, okay," he said. "I have some straightening up to do with my books and papers."

So here I am at the library, overlooking a green, manicured lawn which leads down to a pond mirroring the trees beyond. My mother-in-law is coming. The house is in order. How did my cluttered, topsy-turvy life come to this point? It began when my kitchen sink cabinets rotted.

In other words, I reflected the attitude of the newsman in the movie *Network* who shouted, "I'm mad as hell and I'm not going to take it anymore." When the embarrassment, frustration, and anger go, they are replaced by a steel-cold determination to change. And we do.

What's peculiar about this whole story is that my long-suffering husband at times still carries the fear born of years of living with things out of control. It shows how hard it is on everybody to live that way.

"It is always darkest before the dawn." The reason this is true is because we can stand only so much darkness. Then we *make* the dawn come; we insist that it come. Are you ready to make the dawn come? To insist on it coming? Not to rest until it comes—and soon? That's desire. We must have it.

Thoughts are powerful things. We make our own situations by our own thinking. Like a genie, materializing from a cloud in a bottle, our thoughts turn into the life we see before us. Thoughts are indiscriminate. They work positively as well as negatively. If you direct them toward neatness, the house will materialize in an orderly way. If you don't direct your thoughts toward neatness, the empty space will be filled with disordered thoughts and the house will materialize in that way. Your desire to live in beauty and order is significant. If you can conceive it, you can achieve it.

Go back to the six practical steps at the beginning of this chapter. It is very important that you follow them exactly so that your mind will conceive clearly the goals you wish to achieve.

You will not always find clear sailing. There will be discouragements and failures. Don't let that stop you. Every failure carries an equivalent seed of success.

There is another you, different from the one you have been living with. She is a successful, powerful person in her house. She is your other self, not a new self. She's been there all along. Your other self has the ability and power to obtain beauty and order.

Be open-minded about yourself. Open your mind to the possibility of success. It will come.

Now It's Your Turn

The six strategic steps to accomplishing what you want are:

1. Decide exactly what you want.
2. Decide what you will do to get it.
3. Set a time limit.
4. Make a plan.
5. Make the steps definite by writing them down.
6. Read aloud the statements you have just written twice a day.

Use the following space to outline your own goals.

Step 1. My goals include:

_____

_____

_____

_____

_____

Step 2. In order to achieve my goals, I am willing to: (What changes in my life am I willing to make?)

_____

_____

_____

_____

Step 3. I will reach my goals by: (Use specific dates; be realistic.)

_____

_____

_____

_____

_____

Step 4. In order to reach my goal, I plan to:

_____

_____

_____

_____

Step 5. You just did it!

Step 6. Read the above out loud twice a day—when you get up in the morning and when you go to bed at night. You're on your way!

9

Rethink Your Position

Thoughts rule the world.
RALPH WALDO EMERSON

Whatever we tell ourselves consistently and repeatedly becomes a part of us whether it is true or not. Once it becomes a part of us it begins to become true. Because thoughts are so powerful, they can make things happen. Once they take root, they grow and attract thoughts of the same kind. Soon the mass of thought grows to an overpowering force. If we convince ourselves something can be done, it will be done. It must be done. It is already done. We just need to follow through on effecting it.

Let me use an example. I have a strange problem with my weight. Apparently my mind approves of my body weighing ten pounds more than the rational part of me wants it to. I know this is true because the last time I weighed myself I saw that I had lost about four pounds. *That only leaves six more to lose,* I told myself. However, I noticed that another self somewhere in another part of my mind was saying, *That means you can eat more. You have four pounds you can gain and still be okay.*

I suppose we all have ambivalent feelings about certain things. On the one hand, I want to weigh six pounds less and on the other I feel I can weigh four pounds more.

Concerning the house, on the one hand I want to have a beautiful, orderly house and on the other I want to live a casual, disorderly life. The question is "Which one will win?" The answer is, the one whose thought process is stronger.

As for my weight, I have found a wonderful way to tip the scale of desire the way I want it to go. I use an autosuggestion tape to reinforce my goals. I reaffirm to myself twice a day that I want to lose six pounds. My weight slowly, but surely, begins to drop.

The self-hypnosis tape is nothing more than a way to concentrate on reaffirming my desire and my plan for weight loss. Listening to that tape is one of the nice things I do for myself. It helps me be the person I really want to be.

Denis Waitley, in his book *Seeds of Greatness* (Revell, 1983), suggests that people use this repetition to reinforce thinking that will help them achieve their goals. He has found that "self-talk" statements recorded on an audio-cassette tape in the person's own voice against a background of slow baroque music are very significant helps.

To make a tape, write your self-talk down, go to a quiet place, play slow baroque music, and read your statement aloud to yourself in a normal voice. Make your statement personal by using the words *I, me,* and *my.* Make them affirming statements in the present tense such as:

I am relaxing.

I feel my muscles growing relaxed and warm.

My breathing is regular.

My heartbeat is slow.

I am entering a state of relaxation.

I am a person of great dignity.

I am a person of significant worth.

It is good to be alive.

I make many good contributions to the world.

I feel happy and positive about my life.

My house is beautiful and orderly.

I am relaxed and happy.

I enjoy being here.

The sunshine and breezes enliven my life and home.

I am excited about the opportunities in life and what I am accomplishing.

My home is beautiful and orderly.

Being in my home gives me strength and energy.

I thank God for my life and this day.

Repeat each statement three times. The music should be slightly louder than your voice. The self-talk should be clearly audible, but not dominant. As you listen, feel the joy of success.

As you relax, your mind will accept the statements you are making. You are not lying to yourself. You are simply listening to your "other self," the one who wants you to have a lovely house and to reach all your goals.

You and I are always talking to ourselves, whether we do it with a tape recorder or not. Frequently, we think negative, destructive thoughts that make us weak and ineffective. Messies in particular, being high-quality performance people, must keep telling themselves positive things lest they mislead themselves. Using this method, you will make sure that your thoughts are the right thoughts.

However you do it, whether by reading your goals aloud to yourself twice a day as mentioned in chapter 8, or making a self-talk tape, or purchasing an autosuggestion tape, definite repeated retraining of your thoughts is essential to success.

I was listening to a very successful man being interviewed on the radio. When asked the secret of success, he said that during his childhood, his father encouraged him to memorize a little poem. Through the years, this poem ran through his brain affirming and reaffirming that success was possible even when it seemed impossible. Although others discouraged him, he was successful in attaining his goals. He attributed it in large part to this poem.

It Couldn't Be Done

Somebody said that it couldn't be done,
　　But he with a chuckle replied,
That "maybe it couldn't," but he would be one
　　Who wouldn't say so till he'd tried.
So he buckled right in with the trace of a grin
　　On his face. If he worried he hid it.
He started to sing as he tackled the thing
　　That couldn't be done, and he did it.

EDGAR A. GUEST

Each time he was challenged, that little ditty ran through his brain. His father had given him a great gift—the gift of powerful thoughts. These lead to definite purpose and plans. Applied with persistence, they culminate in success.

In order to cement your desire further, you need outside reinforcement. A great deal of strength is found in working with others. Coals that are separate lose their heat much faster than coals all piled together. You *can* make the change alone; however, it is so much better if you find another person to succeed with. This is one case where one plus one equals more than two. Somehow the bond between those striving together for a goal becomes a third power. If you have more than two in a self-help group working positively together for a goal, you have a very strong power for change. Messies Anonymous self-help groups are designed to put this force for good to work for you. It only takes two or three to make a self-help group.

For those who do not have a self-help group in their area and don't wish to start one, letter writing may be a catalyst for success. Many important plans have been formulated and born through letters. The idea for the unification of the thirteen colonies was begun through correspondence among those who were later to lead the revolution. If writing appeals to you, write to a Messie you know who wants to reform. If you need to find a pen pal, send for the Messies Anonymous "Connections" list of those who wish to correspond. If you'd like information about starting a self-help group or if you would like a copy of this M.A. "Connections" list, send a stamped, self-addressed, legal-sized envelope to Messies Anonymous, Department B, 5025 S.W. 114th Avenue, Miami, Florida 33165. Include a word or two about yourself so we can add you to the list.

Retraining our thinking so that a messy house becomes unacceptable and only a beautiful orderly house is acceptable to our way of thinking is imperative. Only a real change in thinking will produce the persistence we need to keep on when the going gets tough—and it *will* get tough.

There will be times when you think you can't keep on, that it is not worth it. There will be times when family and friends will criticize you for how or what you are doing. There will be times when their lack of cooperation will be discouraging.

You will give yourself many excuses for quitting:

I don't have enough energy.

I don't have enough time.

I don't have enough desire.

My house is too small.

My house is too large.

My family is too messy.

A strong desire to change will keep a reforming Messie going when these discouragements come. Without persistence, there will be no success.

Remember the chapter title "Victor or Victim: It's Really Up to You"? You are the only one who can make it happen. Your desire to change is newborn at this time. Feed it, strengthen it, protect it, so it will grow into a strong, persistent, satisfying way of life.

Close your mind to the possibility of failure. When I first started changing, I was tempted many times to quit and go back. But I didn't because that old way of life was so painful to me. I was *determined* never to live that way again. Only that kind of determined attitude along with solid retraining of thinking will insure success.

10

Active Duty or Why Messies Are So Busy

Never before have we had so little time in which to do so much.

FRANKLIN D. ROOSEVELT

Most Messies are very busy people. We dash from activity to project to activity and back, anxious to fill our hours with worthwhile pursuits. A few super-organized people might be able to keep a schedule like this without having their lives come all unraveled. Messies cannot. Born into the world with characteristics that make organizing difficult, Messies' lives stagger under this kind of schedule.

Why do we work so hard? Why do we keep ourselves so very busy?

There are several reasons, some of which are all right; others which are not.

Pride

The busier we are, the more highly regarded we are in our society. When we enter a doctor's office that is crowded to the rafters, our admiration for the doctor is reinforced. We may have to wait too long and the doctor may be stretched beyond his capacity to perform well because of overscheduling, but we still think, *He must be such a good doctor; look how busy he is.*

Busyness means we are needed; we are wanted. Pride of the wrong kind, the desire to impress others above all, pushes us to behave foolishly. Our schedules, our personal lives, our genuinely good activities suffer. People may notice and admire us. Busyness is encouraged by society. But what a price we have paid to have our egos boosted!

Laziness

It takes effort to organize my time. It takes energy. It takes discipline for a Messie who loves to please to say no to someone who asks for time and energy for their needy activity. This may include our children and our husbands as well. Certainly, we may help others and should. But only within the boundaries predetermined by us. We must set our own schedule in accordance with our priorities. We must accept only the activities that fit into our schedule.

Gordon McDonald, in his very excellent book, *Ordering Your Private World* (Moody Press, 1984), tells of how he took command of his time schedule. It all revolves around his calendar. Eight weeks in advance, he blocks in his personal schedule. He schedules time for reading, time for meditation, time to be with his family and friends, and time for study.

When he has requests for his time, he consults his calendar. If the time requested has already been blocked out for himself, he asks for an alternative time, one that fits his plans better. He sets his priorities for the use of his time early. Other plans flow around those priorities.

It would be so much easier from the planning standpoint to just do whatever comes up day by day—to respond to the immediate, to the demands of other people. That is the lazy way. It is also the nonproductive way. We won't have time to do the work important to us, and that includes the house.

Enthusiasm for Life

Messies are generally very creative, outgoing, enthusiastic people. We tend to overdo, to be too expansive in our living. Like children in a toy store, we view life as chocked full of wonderful activities and opportunities for us to enjoy. We want to be involved in hobbies, crafts, and fine arts. We can't pass up the opportunity for reading and seminars. Of course, our children's activities are so important and fun, we must get involved. Like that child in the toy store, we gather into our schedules all of the activities that attract our ebullient attention. We forget that there will come a time when we'll have to pay. Nothing is free. We pay for these activities with time and energy. If we pay too much for them, we don't have time and energy left for the essentials of life. As a result, the family may have to eat one more lick-and-promise meal, the unwashed dishes will wait a little longer, and we begin to cut back on the basics that determine our quality of life. Without a quality life in which the home and family are cared for properly, these other good activities lose their luster.

A peculiar thing begins to happen as the home front deteriorates. We begin to search for more activities outside the home. Who wants to spend time there? We begin to daydream and read. As a result, a downward spiral develops, and the home suffers more and more.

We know we are overbusy when we forget appointments, lose things, fail to return important calls, put things in piles until we get to them, let deadlines for things like driver's licenses or tag renewals slide, forget to record checks, and spend time doing small nonessential things just to make ourselves believe we are trying to get things in order. For instance, an overbusy person will spend her time cleaning the oven when the kitchen is a shambles and then wonder at the end of the day why the house looks so bad after she worked so hard. We jump from one activity to another trying to make a dent.

Soon the stress of the way of life we have created begins to take its toll. We become nervous because things are out of control. We have an uncomfortable feeling that we may be in trouble and not know it. Has the driver's license lapsed? Or the insurance? Could we find the Band-Aids if a child got cut? Have we put that refund check in some pile or thrown it away by mistake? Did we forget and leave clothes in the washer soaking? Do the children have clean clothes for school tomorrow? We begin waking up early just to worry.

The family becomes nervous, too. When the children have to hunt and hope for their clothes and, as a consequence, miss the school bus, they are upset. When the check bounces because we let the banking get confused, our husband is upset. When these incidents multiply, it becomes a nightmare.

Personal relationships begin to unravel because we are overbusy. Our conversations become mere reacting instead of satisfying communication. Messies cannot handle a heavy or nonplanned schedule. We must cut back on our activities until we find the level of unbusyness in which we can maintain a quality life. Perhaps you will need to cut way back at first and slowly add a few activities at a time. Always add with care.

There is one type of Messie who is not overbusy. She is suffering busy-burnout. This Messie may have tried so hard and so long without success that she has quit trying. Perhaps she is so traumatized she is immobilized by depression. No more busy schedule for her. She has quit and simply withdrawn from it all.

For the still overbusy Messie and the one who has quit, there is one commonality: Both feel a gut-level, heartrending dissatisfaction with themselves. Life is no fun anymore. The busy Messie doesn't take time to admit it. The withdrawn Messie suppresses it. But the dissatisfaction is there and must be highlighted before any help comes. Until we see how much this overbusy way of life is hurting us, we won't stop it.

When we decide to cut out many of the busywork activities, just as we get rid of unnecessary stuff by the Mount Vernon method, it is hard to decide what activities to discard. Some Messies will insist that they are doing only the bare minimum now, only the essentials. When they look for something to do away with, nothing can go. All of the activities seem so essential. We must do them all.

Let me tell you my experience. When my daughter, Lucy, was a newborn infant, just home from the hospital, she developed a distressing habit. She had trouble going to sleep and staying asleep. I took time from my busy schedule to rock her to sleep and put her into her crib, only to be recalled by a startled, screaming baby a few minutes later.

You must understand that I had determined earlier that the baby would not slow me down. I would be Mrs. Superwoman. I could do it all. This sleep problem was certainly challenging that. My important plans were suffering.

In desperation I called Dr. Wilson. We lived in rural

northern Indiana at the time. The phone lines were old. A call to Dr. Wilson a few miles down the road in Columbia City was long-distance. The connection was bad. Loudly, I explained the problem.

"IT SEEMS LIKE SHE IS HAVING NIGHTMARES," I shouted.

"SHE MAY BE," he crackled across the line, and then he went on to prescribe help for the problem.

"DR. WILSON!" I said, trying to be heard, "I MUST NOT HAVE HEARD YOU CLEARLY. IT SOUNDED LIKE YOU SAID THAT I OUGHT TO HOLD THE BABY FOR *EIGHT HOURS A DAY.*"

"THAT'S WHAT I DID SAY. I BELIEVE THAT WILL SOLVE THE PROBLEM," he replied only too clearly.

All my busyness came to a screeching halt. Baby and I certainly got a lot of rest. She slept and I watched TV. We were both happier and calmer. My busy schedule went to pot. We were both better for it.

Perhaps you have had times when your busy schedule was interrupted by a broken arm or by having to leave town for an emergency. Surprisingly, things do not destruct without you. In most cases, things continue very well in your absence. (When others know you won't be there to do your jobs, they step in and do them.) Cutting back on your schedule is a little like a vacation. People get along without you then, don't they? You really don't *have* to do it all. The trick when you're not on vacation is to make sure others know that you expect them to begin taking over if they want jobs to be done.

We must do a Mount Vernoning of our schedules. Get rid of all the activities that are cluttering up our lives. We give away unwanted clothes, don't we? Now let's give those unwanted activities to someone else or just throw them out entirely. What a relief it will be!

When our lives begin to right themselves from the topsy-turvy mess they are in now, we will be calmer and happier. We will have confidence that our lives are under control. The best thing is that we will then have quality time for ourselves—to read, to think, to plan, to dream. On my key chain I have these words from eighteenth-century poet William Cowper:

> A life all turbulence and noise may seem
> > To him that leads it wise and to be praised.
> But wisdom is a pearl with most success
> > Sought in still waters.

lit·tle min·utes/lit-əl min-əts short periods of time generally left over from or in the middle of larger projects. "Little minutes" occur when your ride is late, when dinner is ready but the kids aren't home, when you're stuck in line or in a traffic jam or in a waiting room. The most popular example of "little minutes" is a television commercial during which most Americans have learned to fix a three-minute snack. Other examples include making the bed while waiting for the coffee to brew, writing letters while waiting for an appointment, rinsing the sink and wiping the mirror while waiting for the curling iron to heat, washing dishes while waiting for the family to gather for dinner. Used effectively, "little minutes" reap many hours of pleasure and relaxation.

Hurry Up and Wait— Why Time Management Techniques Don't Work

Procrastination is the art of keeping up with yesterday.
DONALD ROBERT PERRY MARQUIS

The book market is full of books on time management but they won't help the Messie whose problem is procrastination. She will just procrastinate putting the time-management techniques into use. The reason is that procrastinators really want to procrastinate for reasons they themselves do not usually understand.

Procrastinators have a distorted sense of time. Actually, they live apart from the restraints of time to some extent. I do not wear a watch and almost never know the date. I only check the time or date when it seems important for me to know them. My judgment of when it is important is not always accurate. That is why I almost missed the opening day of school.

Time passes erratically for the Messie procrastinator. Usually time goes more slowly for the Messie than for other people so she is surprised to find she has procrastinated so long. Occasionally, time speeds up, unexpectedly. When she thought she had enough time to do a job, she finds the time has passed by too quickly to get the job done. So a deadline is missed.

Procrastinators suffer from a complexity of thinking that works against their doing what really is in their best interest to do. They also generally suffer from a feeling of low self-esteem. Procrastinating is one way of protecting their self-worth from being lowered.

Messie procrastinators also feel, conversely, that they are very capable people and that they are capable of accomplishing many excellent goals if they could just "get it together." If pushed, they might confess they have thoughts of greatness or genius in certain areas. They are perfectionists in their own way.

Because they are perfectionists, Messies take a long time to decide *what* to do. Then after they decide what to do, they wait a little longer to see whether or not anything comes up to cancel the wisdom of that decision. All of this mulling things over takes time. This kind of procrastination seems rational to the careful Messie who is already low in self-esteem. She doesn't want to make a mistake.

The low self-esteem and perfectionism combine to make a recipe for failure. Let's look at several examples of how this works.

Joan wants to upgrade her house by redecorating, so she spends hours looking through sale catalogs, browsing in stores, and visiting model homes. She's been at this project for some time, but the house is still waiting for the wonderful transformation. Why? Joan is not sure of her decorating ability or her ability to maintain a beautiful house. As a substitute for doing the decorating, she talks about her big plans, she shows catalogs and magazine cutouts as proof of her sincerity. Because she is afraid of failure, she never actually *does* the job. She can't be criticized for doing a poor job if she never really does it. She tells herself she has to get the house straightened up before she begins beautifying it. Here we see a combination of her poor self-esteem and perfectionism. Her procrastination has shielded her self-esteem from being hurt.

Mary, another procrastinator, wants to get her house in order. She feels she must, however, do some other things first. *People see the outside of the house more often than the inside,* she tells herself as she does what she knows how to do well—

yardwork. No one would guess how the inside of the house looks. She never fails at the job she does on the inside because she never starts it. She's too busy in the yard. She tells herself that if she ever did get to the house, it would be beautifully maintained. After all, isn't the beautiful yard proof of that? On those occasions when guests are invited, Mary starts late and does a quick surface job to make the public area look okay. She tells herself that if she had had the time to do it, the house would have been thoroughly cleaned. She did not fail to keep the house nice—lack of time was the problem. Procrastination has protected her self-esteem. She has a fear of failure. Mary's true ability in the house has never been tested. She avoids trying so she can avoid failure. She has an *illusion* of ability.

People also procrastinate because of fear of success.

For various reasons, Messie procrastinators sometimes sabotage their own success. We may tell ourselves several things.

"Perhaps the kids and my husband would feel it wasn't 'home' anymore."

"What would I do with my time—why would I even be needed at the house—if everything got caught up?"

"If I get the house under control and keep it nice, people will begin to expect it and I might begin to slip back into my old ways. It's too much pressure to keep it up."

"I am a Messie, a wonderful, creative, procrastinating Messie. If I succeed in the house and things are neat, my creativity will be stifled."

"Mother, bless her heart, is such a Messie. Like mother, like daughter. It is a bond between us. I don't want to make Mom feel bad."

"Mom is such a perfectionist in the house. Even though I'm grown, my messiness keeps me dependent on

97

**I'LL THINK ABOUT IT TOMORROW—
AFTER ALL, TOMORROW IS ANOTHER DAY**

her like a child. If I get control of the house, I'll have to take my place in the adult world."

So sometimes we procrastinate in the house because we fear the changes success might bring.

Jodie has a messy house. Her mom is always after her to fix it up. Her husband and kids complain, but the house stays messy. Jodie is a capable adult woman. She feels that she should control her own actions and not be controlled by others; so she says no to their pleas. To her it is a sign of power. Any imposed schedule is a challenge to be defeated. As a matter of fact, it may be that this rebellious attitude toward being dominated accounts for Messies ignoring time. *I will do what I want, when I want. I will defeat the restraints of time,* she thinks deep in her heart. It gives her a feeling of power and control but is disastrous as far as success is concerned.

This rebellious attitude may also make the Messie procrastinator impervious to the restraints of the usual housekeeping rules. *Other people may need to put things away but not me! I'll keep everything out. I can remember which pile it is in. It will be so much easier to get to. I can handle it.*

I remember a woman in an organization workshop I attended saying she had a mirror that sat on the floor waiting to be hung for years. But she wasn't going to hang it because it bugged her mother so much that she didn't.

Sometimes people procrastinate paying bills out of resentment. They feel the taxes or utilities are too high or they don't like the doctor's treatment so they make them wait for their money.

When the Messie procrastinator begins to see that all of this procrastination is painful and hurts self-esteem more than protects it, she begins to consider changing. But how?

It is important to set specific goals and to commit ourselves to them aloud to some sympathetic person. The Messie procrastinator likes to make vague, general grand plans for change. This makes accomplishing the goal *vague* and *general.* However, it is important to set very specific, easily observable goals which have a time target.

When you tell your goals and time target to the sympathetic person you choose to help you, also tell her the steps you are going to take to accomplish your goal. Messies must learn to look specifically at the job to be done.

When the Messie first begins to change it is hard, because Messies appreciate only final accomplishments, not intermediate steps to the final goals. It is important to value each step toward the final goal.

In the same grand way of thinking, Messies want to work only when they have large blocks of time to work in. A few minutes here and there are disregarded as unimportant when they actually could be just the time needed to get many jobs started and well on the way. Frequently, a big job can be conquered by doing it in short time segments such as five or fifteen minutes. When the set time limit is up, the work stops. Messies find it hard to start doing things this way.

It may be that Messies like large blocks of time because they feel they cannot be jumping from one activity to another—that is not a productive way to work.

Messies learn to fear this fitful, distractible way of working. They are aware that in the past they have found themselves unaccountably jumping from one job to another, not following through on any. This is frustrating and unproductive, so Messies tend to avoid short-term jobs. Messies have to concentrate so hard on a job to get it done that it is hard for them to shift gears to another job.

The difference between being distracted and this plan I am proposing of using "little minutes" to get a job started or to continue on a job is that in the latter case using little minutes is deliberately done. Using little minutes productively and deliberately is a skill learned by many people who are very accomplished producers.

Another reason Messies don't like to do small jobs is because it takes a Messie more time and effort than most people to take out and put away any items needed for a job. It does not seem worthwhile. For instance, the Messie procrastinator may have lost the bills, or the pen, or the checkbook to pay the bills. The Messie procrastinator may not be able to find the dustcloth and spray wax to do a quick polish job on the living room furniture, or the envelopes or stamps to send a quick letter. To Messies, all jobs are big jobs, so we procrastinate. It is imperative that the Messie procrastinator set up the house so she can quickly get her hands on whatever she needs to do jobs easily.

Because Messies are perfectionists and have a low self-esteem, they are easily discouraged. Any problems they run into make them feel stupid or dumb so they retreat to their old standby against failure—procrastination.

To experience success in overcoming these problems, the Messie procrastinator can be helped by special support either from an understanding friend or a support group. Messies Anonymous support groups or "Connections" writing partners may be just the help needed.

Knowing the roots of our procrastination may help to weaken the hold these roots have on our lives. It is not noble to be a perfectionist. It is just an excuse not to work. Fear of success, fear of failure, and a rebellious attitude of self-assertion all work to hurt us. We must change our attitude about our former behaviors.

The real key is to build a realistic picture of ourselves as people who are valuable even when we try and do not achieve. Remember, we are people of dignity. We don't need to protect ourselves from failure by procrastinating.

William Knaus, an expert on the problems of procrastination says,

The object [of changing attitudes] is to help people create an image of themselves as doers; not stewers. They have to overcome their self-doubts and build tolerance for frustration. Too many people just don't want to put themselves out. They think somebody will take over for them or bail them out (U.S. News and World Report, October 24, 1984, p. 11).

Spotting and Untying Organizational Knots

A. Put a check to the left side of any areas in your life that are not organized—where you think further control is needed.

___ 1. Finding things (Glasses, keys, purse, etc.). ___

___ 2. Meal planning and preparation. ___

___ 3. Cleaning the house. ___

___ 4. Paper (Finding, filing, and sorting). ___

___ 5. Keeping finances in order. ___

___ 6. Laundry (Washing, drying, folding, and putting it away). ___

___ 7. Keeping things picked up. ___

___ 8. Dishes (Washing, drying, and putting away immediately). ___

___ 9. Grocery shopping. ___

___ 10. Delegating jobs. ___

___ 11. Being on time. ___

___ 12. OTHERS

___ _____

___ _____

B. Put the letters of the category below that *best* explains the reason for lack of organization in the area that you checked. Put the letters to the right of the category in the space provided.

LF   Lack of Follow Through—Getting the main part of the job done but failing to finish it up.

LP   Lack of Planning—Not planning for the future. Maybe you prefer spontaneous living.

AD   Lack of Attention to Detail—Thinking only in terms of the "big picture."

IP   Impatience with Paper Work—Easily frustrated.

PT   Perfectionistic Thinking—Finding it hard to decide the best way to do the job.

PG   Orientation toward *Present* Gratification—Wishing to have it easy now, even though it will make the future harder.

TC   Too Compliant—Letting others dictate what you do and letting others ignore your plans.

EC   Excessive Confusion—The situation is so complicated and confused that it is difficult to begin.

C. Describe in your own words what keeps you from getting organized.

12

Special Tactics

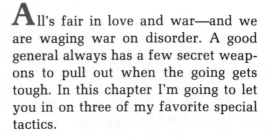

All's fair in love and war—and we are waging war on disorder. A good general always has a few secret weapons to pull out when the going gets tough. In this chapter I'm going to let you in on three of my favorite special tactics.

The Maid and I

In Messie days of yore, I would occasionally have a maid come help around the house. I found it helpful to have someone who could swoop in, bring order and some degree of clean, and swoop out again. For about half a day things would be so nice and then gloom would descend slowly as clutter crept out into my orderly house. Dirty dishes would creep into the sink, dirty laundry would sneak into the hall, and shoes would appear under the living room sofa.

And then there was always the problem of preparing for the maid. A certain amount of cleaning and straightening must be done. The piles needed to be somewhat corralled before she could come. Getting ready for the maid was no small job in itself.

One of my seminar attendees said that a maid she shared with some other ladies in the neighborhood charged her five dollars more to do her house because of the clutter. This incident was the catalyst that made her finally decide to find some way of making a change. In almost each seminar I give I have a maid attend. In my last seminar I had a lady who founded and ran a maid service. Just because you can clean another person's house does not mean you can organize yourself.

I was more prepared one Saturday recently when I called a local maid service and asked them to send a maid. I asked for a fast thorough one. They sent Debbie. I wanted to be there when she came to show her the products to use, where they were, and how I wanted things done. For six hours she was there. I wondered when we started how she could fill six hours. But she did! And I worked with her much of the time. Beds were moved and floors mopped and waxed. Everything was vacuumed. Furniture and cabinets were dusted and waxed.

I found out two things. In some areas I did the work better than she did. In some areas she was better than I was. We worked well as a team, and a lot of behind-the-scenes cleaning got done. I was pleased. The price was high, but it was, for that time, worth it. It was a lot better than the time I hired a maid to come clean while I was gone and my husband was home. I told him what to tell her to do because my mother was coming for a visit and *something had to be done.* When I arrived home from work, I found she had cleaned the stove very well—but little else. That was a disaster.

Perhaps my experience can offer some guidelines if you are searching for a maid.

1. Decide whether you want a slow but thorough maid or a fast surface cleaner or a combination of the two and make your preference known before you hire her.

2. Be prepared to work with her the first time. There are so many ways to do things and each house has its peculiarities, so you need to guide her in your way for your house.

3. I had never used a maid service before but found this experience very satisfactory. You might inquire if there

is one in your area. You will find them in the yellow pages under *Maids*. If you want heavier cleaning done such as windows, rugs, etc., call a company under *Cleaning Services*, which advertises they do residential work.

4. Don't be too picky. I thought she left too much water on the floor after she mopped. But don't let your perfection make you tune out any help from a maid.

Now the clincher. My husband doesn't generally want to be bothered with a change in his routine by having a maid come. He was not sure it would be worth the money. (I had to sort of ease Debbie in over his grumbling.) Last night, *he* suggested it would be nice to have her come back in a month or so.

Miracles do happen.

BADARACCO

The Flipper

In chapter 2 I explained the Mount Vernon method for organizing your house. But any Messie knows that the real problem is not getting the house in order—it's *keeping* it that way. The Flipper is the heart of the Messies Anonymous organizational program.

Let's think of the Flipper as a recipe for a cake.

When you get through with your recipe, you will have twenty-four cards set in a book.

At one sitting you decide your cleaning schedule. On each of these cards you put a few of the jobs you would like to get done during the week. Spread them all out so everything doesn't pile up for Saturday. Each day, look at the Flipper and do the jobs indicated. Like all good ideas, it is simple. For Messies to use it efficiently, it has to be simple.

This is the basic idea of the Flipper.

Now let's get back to the recipe.

Ingredients:

One small photo album. The kind that has twenty-four plastic sleeves with blank cards in the sleeves. These clear plastic sleeves are supposed to hold snapshots but we are going to put in cards listing our housecleaning chores.

One Vis-a-Vis pen. You can buy these at any office supply store. Get the fine line if you have a choice. Use this pen to mark off the jobs as you do them each day. The pen marks will wipe off easily so you can use the Flipper again and again after you finish going through it the first time.

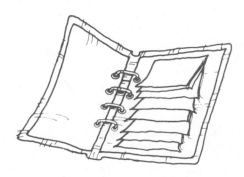

One paper clip. Preferably plastic, because metal rusts. Put that on the card you are working on because Messies have poor memories. If we forget which card we're on, being perfectionists, we won't want to continue until we remember just exactly which one it was.

This brings up the problem of what to do when you get behind. You have two choices:

1. You can try to get caught up to where you should be.

2. You can forget about what you have neglected and start from the day you would be on if you had kept up.

The correct answer is number 2. Forget about what you neglected. Start from whatever day it is. The Alcoholics Anonymous creed of living "one day at a time" applies here. Forget the past. Start today and make today a success.

Some paper and a pen. Perhaps a pencil will be better because you'll change your mind as you think.

Write down the jobs you would like to accomplish twice a week. Put those on the appropriate cards. For example, if you wish to mop the kitchen floor twice a week, put that down on first-week Tuesday and Friday cards, second-week Tuesday and Friday cards, and third-week Tuesday and Friday cards.

Then select the jobs you wish to do once a week. Write those on the three cards for the day you choose, say Wednesday of each of the three weeks.

Next decide which jobs you wish to do only once every three weeks. Choose any convenient days from the cards to do that job. Write each job down. Now you are finished with the day-of-the-week cards.

This is the basic cake. Now for the filling.

There are some jobs you would like to do daily. There should be no more than six or seven. These do not go on the day-of-the-week cards; they go on three daily cards. Don't include jobs that are already a habit.

All these cards represent three weeks of housework. One card will be Monday, first week; then Tuesday, first week, and so on, until the first week is finished. The second and third weeks follow consecutively. Notice there is no Sunday because everybody needs one day a week off, at least. You may choose Sunday and/or any other day you want.

1st Week	Menu
1st Week	Daily
1st Week	Monday
1st Week	Tuesday
1st Week	Wednesday
1st Week	Thursday
1st Week	Friday
1st Week	Saturday
2nd Week	Menu
2nd Week	Daily
2nd Week	Monday
2nd Week	Tuesday

2nd Week	Wednesday
2nd Week	Thursday
2nd Week	Friday
2nd Week	Saturday
3rd Week	Menu
3rd Week	Daily
3rd Week	Monday
3rd Week	Tuesday
3rd Week	Wednesday
3rd Week	Thursday
3rd Week	Friday
3rd Week	Saturday

Cards which are located at the beginning of each set of weekday cards look like this:

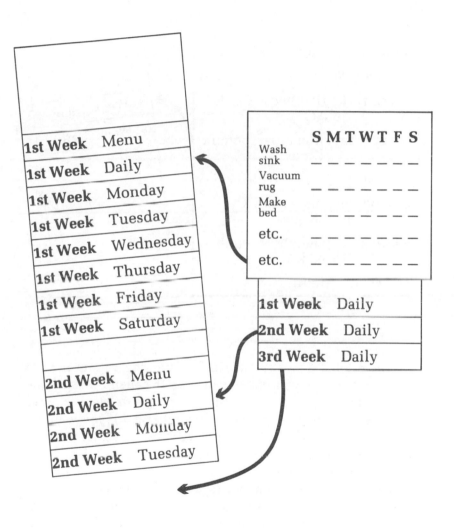

We've got the cake and filling. Now we need the icing. You will notice that the card above the daily card is empty. Use that for your menu planning. Decide what schedule of eating you want, write it down, and slip it into the sleeve above the daily.

Sunday: Chicken, rice, peas

Monday: Tuna casserole, salad

Tuesday: Chili, cheese toast, Jell-O

Wednesday: Meat loaf, potato, limas

Thursday: Quiche, fruit

Friday: Fish, macaroni & cheese, peas

Saturday: Spaghetti, French bread, slaw

1st Week   Menu

1st Week Menu

1st Week Daily

The cake is almost ready. Just a little decoration and we are done. Perhaps you did not include the menu or perhaps your photo album has more than twenty-four sleeves. Add motivational sayings from this or any other book you want.

Now your recipe is finished and ready to use. Don't, I repeat, DO NOT use the Flipper until you have finished the Mount Vernon method.

The Mount Vernon method is done only one time to get the house in order. The Flipper is used to *keep* the house in order. Use the Flipper regularly, erasing the marks when it is full and going back through it again and again.

Like all good recipes, you may share with your family. Let them do and check off jobs from the Flipper. Working together, you can do it. I know you can!

Journaling—The Ultimate Memory

It is important to keep in mind that being a Messie does not mean just having a disordered house. A Messie has certain personal characteristics that lead her into a disordered way of life. These characteristics will never be eliminated nor should they be. Many of our personal characteristics are not bad, they are just misapplied or overdone. You do not need to change into another person to bring order and beauty into your home. You do, however, need to make some appropriate changes in your thinking and behavior in order to make changes in the house and make them permanently.

We take a threefold approach to changing.

1. In the first part of this book, and at points throughout, I have emphasized the intrinsic value of each person. A healthy respect for yourself will compel you to realign your environment to match with your inner beauty.

2. To strengthen that change, you need to use change-making techniques, such as goal setting, retraining of your thought habits, and support from self-help groups.

3. Some of your characteristics need to be rechanneled into neater ways of doing things. That brings me to a topic close to my heart—the journal.

Messies are sentimental people. Many also have poor memories. This makes a very unsettling combination for the Messie. When a Messie who is sentimental knows that the incidents of life which are important to her are apt to fade away, she makes certain adjustments in order to keep them alive in her memory. The most common ways are by keeping mementos, souvenirs, and pictures.

The pictures don't take up much room but the mementos do. Old jewelry, baby clothes, pressed flowers, and many other items that would not usually classify as typical remembrances are kept because they are a part of the past. Slowly our houses fill up with unpleasant heaps. We hate the clutter but we feel that if we let these things go, our past will go with them.

What are the alternatives to collecting all this clutter? The best alternative I have found is to keep a journal.

Journaling is enjoying a comeback in popularity. Before TV, when people had more time, it was a very widely practiced pastime. I remember finding an old journal a stranger had left in the attic of a house my grandparents bought. I wish I had kept it. Once you tune into the idea, you will be surprised at how many people, even today, you will meet or read about who keep journals. Most do not talk about it. It seems to be a secret pastime.

Maybe there is a reason for the secrecy. A journal is a place where one can bare one's soul. It can be an intimate activity in a world where we feel uncomfortable with intimacy. But for Messies, it is the perfect answer to the problem of preserving the past in memory.

Let's talk about how it's done. My journal is a 6″ × 9″, spiral-bound notebook. I bought it in a drugstore, I believe. It's not fancy at all. If you want something a bit nicer, most bookstores have selections of blank books that make wonderful journals. You can get books with lovely fabric bindings or even interesting journals imported from China or Italy. Art stores as well carry a selection of sketch books in a variety of sizes, bindings, and papers which serve as great journals. Use your imagination—after all, you are writing your book.

There are advantages to using a journal instead of one of those little five-year diaries with the lock on the front. If you have a predated diary, you feel compelled to write in it every day. If you don't, you feel guilty. In addition, those little diaries have minuscule spaces for writing. There are two final problems with the five-year, lock-on-the-front diary. One is that you might lose the key if you lock it and the other is that if you lose the diary, you have lost five years of memories.

Almost every day I write in my journal, but if I miss a day or two I don't panic. What do I write? Memories. Memories of the day past. Thoughts. Dreams. Hopes. Successes. Failures. Plans. And prayers. Journals are a wonderful place to sort out your priorities and needs. Some people get very creative, recording poetry and special quotations, even including drawings or gluing in special mementos. Consider your journal an empty canvas awaiting your own personal word paintings. The journal is the ultimate remembrance. Trinkets are only the shell of a memory; the journal contains the heart.

Personally, I write from front to back in the usual way for my regular entries. For special entries such as quotations, books I have read, songs or poems to remember, I write from back to front. When the front and back meet the journal is full and I start a new one.

Do people peek in my diary? I doubt it. My family is so used to seeing me writing, they pay no attention. I keep it beside my bed. If you are afraid people will intrude on yours, keep it hidden. If someone asks what you are doing, tell them that it is part of the Messies Anonymous program for household organization. That should be enough to dampen their curiosity.

You might find that your journal will help you to do the Mount Vernon method more easily. As you discard things, you may wish to record their passing in your journal. For instance, when you give away your maternity clothes (if you're finished with them), record that momentous occasion in the book. Write also, how important those births were to you. Include the significance of the great giveaway. An epoch of your life—the child-bearing years—has ended. It is so much more satisfying to do this than to keep a box of useless clothes in an already crowded spot.

We are Messies. We must learn to live in a satisfactory way with our own personalities. Keep your sentimentality. But keep those memories in a small book, not in piles and boxes which, in the end, muddy the memories you have of today.

Rugged Terrain— Special Problem Areas

PART THREE

13

Dollars & Sense

Caution: The following information is for Money Messies who are prepared to face the serious realities of putting their financial matters in order. Wimps need not apply.

Go directly to jail.
Do not pass GO.
Do not collect $200.
MONOPOLY

This chapter could be serious and minutely detailed, but it's not going to be. Many good books have been written on this subject alone and we could never hope to match their completeness in these matters. What we can do is set up some basic principles in money management, give you some personal tips, and direct you to those places where you will find more detail—when you're ready for it.

If you've read this far, I assume that you are serious about getting your money matters under control. At the same time, you're scared. After all, money is a very scary subject. Many psychologists believe that money is an even more volatile subject than sex. If you think about it, they're probably right. So you are probably right to be scared. But knowledge banishes fear.

Why Do Messies Avoid Setting Their Finances in Order?

There are several reasons.

Keeping money matters in order is not easy. This chapter will not give you effort-free methods of bookkeeping and accounting. But we didn't give you any effort-free methods of housekeeping either, and you conquered that, didn't you?

The fact is, this entire project is probably so complicated that no self-respecting Messie would dare attempt it *unless* she was truly convinced that she was worth it. And face it, when we muddle around trying to find a painless, unique way of avoiding a job, we generally spend more time doing the avoiding than it would take to do the job.

Picture yourself as John Wayne. Get that image in your head. Then hitch up your belt, wipe your brow, and plant your feet. It ain't an easy job, but it's yours. And you're gonna do it.

Keeping your finances in order is not glamorous. You can't invite the neighbors over and bask in their admiration as you can with a clean house. This job above all others is for your benefit alone. As such, it flows from a sense of dignity and self-worth. There are few comforts like the sense of having your finances in order and the knowledge that you and your family are reaching for some of your financial goals. And although the neighbors won't ooh and aah, your children shall arise and call you blessed; your husband also he shall praise thee. (Apologies to the author of Proverbs.)

Money matters are so messy, especially for Messies. Losing records, forgetting bills, avoiding detail work, forgetting that cash you need next week. The list goes on and on. Messies have their own special problems with money. But I'll let you in on a secret: *Cleanies have the same problems!* You'd be surprised at how many Cleanies are Money Messies. Okay, all their little pieces of paper are in one place instead of in the glove compartment, on the refrigerator, and in the drawer by the front door. But they still have trouble making order out of all the bits and pieces that make up life today. So be encouraged! Money Mess is not simply a matter of not caring or being untalented. Finances can be complicated and as such need special attention. So pay attention and prepare to win!

The final excuse for not keeping control is that *we are afraid that we might find out that we really are in trouble financially.*

In the early days of flying, pilots did not have accurate instruments to tell them what the plane was doing, so they learned to fly by the way their derrieres felt on the seats. If there was pressure, they were climbing; if there was little or no pressure, they were dropping. Sometimes their derrieres failed to give them enough information, and they crashed.

Some Messies are adept at using the seat-of-the-pants method of money management. They get a feel of whether the money is flowing in or out. And they hope that they are not about to get an unpleasant surprise and crash.

Pilots who fly by the seat of the pants and Messies who manage their finances by the seat of the pants are always under a certain amount of tension. There is stress in not knowing whether there's enough money to cover a check or whether you'll be able to afford that house. In business this is called "crisis management": you move from one crisis to the next, with no time for planning and no energy for life. When this happens you don't manage the money, it manages you.

It feels better for a pilot to be flying happily along in the clouds, feeling everything is all right, than to know that there's a mountain peak looming ahead. Messies are that way. An unfounded sense of well-being, even with an undercurrent of nervousness, is better than knowing for certain that we are in trouble. If we don't balance our checkbooks then it doesn't matter that we spend more than we make. This attitude is immature, foolish, and unworthy behavior. In kinder terms, you deserve better!

Money Management for Messies

When we start learning anything for the first time, we start with the basics. And in learning money management, Messies need to know the following basics:

There are four key words in money management:

1. *Income*—all the money that comes in, from whatever source. Income provides the means to pay

2. *Expenses*—daily, monthly, annually. The financial commitments that need to be met in order to . . . well, to live.

3. *Budget*—(considered a dirty word in most company). A process by which income and expenses are balanced against each other on a monthly or annual basis.

4. *Cashflow*—a semi-technical term for the movement of money in and out of our lives. Think of a *Budget* as a financial snapshot and *Cashflow* as a financial movie.

There are three Financial Realities:

1. You must meet your financial commitments (pay your bills).

2. You must keep records (because)

3. You must file your taxes.

There are two financial goals:

1. You should plan.

2. You should save.

What most concerns us is coping with Financial Realities. If we get these in order, then Financial Goals will begin to emerge as a natural outgrowth. So let's begin.

Reality #1. We must meet our financial commitments. In other words, pay our bills. Of course we must, you say. How utterly obvious. But for a Messie, paying bills can be a nightmare, for several reasons.

- *The bills are missing.* One of the first lessons a Messie learns is to find a place for things. As you've Mount Vernoned your house you've no doubt run across bills in every conceivable place. And by now you've probably herded them toward a central location: a drawer, a desk top, a shoe box. Now is the time to find a place for your finances. You need a place in which there is space to work, space to store records (more on this later), and a space for unpaid bills. Some people use a basket on top of the desk, some people post them on a bulletin board with the due date marked prominently, others simply use the first folder in their file. But you need a place. And you need to keep the Current Unpaid Bills together. When you get a bill, open it. Immediately throw away everything but the bill and the return envelope. Then put it with the rest of the Current Unpaid Bills.

  If you are a visual person—that is, if something is out of sight, then it is truly out of mind—then you must keep the bills in a place where you can see them. This helps avoid the second reason bills are not paid.

- *I forgot.* You may laugh, but to a Money Messie, this is a very real problem. That's why it's important that you have a place for these things, and important that you set aside a special time to do your financial chores: pay bills, do your filing, balance your checkbook, and so on. Pick the same time all the time. Some experts recommend once a month (for example, the first Tuesday of every month), others recommend weekly (you probably will spend less time in the long run if you maintain it that regularly), others find it simply easier to do right after payday (that's when you have the money to pay the bills, right?). At that time you should review your finances, dole out allowances and living expenses, pay your bills, file the paid bills, and balance your checkbook. Which brings us to the third reason that bills are not paid.

- *The checkbook is a mess.* Now if there is only one piece of counsel that you take away from this chapter (assuming that you are still reading), make it this: MAKE FRIENDS WITH YOUR CHECKBOOK. And this is where courage, determination, and discipline come in. Remember John Wayne? "It's a dirty job, but someone's got to do it."

Why? Because your checkbook is the key to restoring order to your money mess. Your checkbook not only tracks the majority of your expense payments, but it also helps you determine what kind of expense it is (which helps in planning), whether the expense is tax deductible (which helps in preparing tax returns), and most importantly, gives you an up-to-the-minute report on your financial situation. There is probably nothing else in your life that gives you so much pertinent information in such a compact form.

"But I hate my checkbook! Things keep getting lost and I'm terrible at subtraction and my husband won't cooperate and I swear my hamster eats a minimum of one check a month. I can't do it!!" Okay—but you couldn't keep an orderly house when you started either, and now look at you! The key is to begin, then keep plugging away, and keep remembering—you deserve an orderly checking account.

CHECKBOOK RULES
Always record the check.
Always record the deposits.
Always reconcile your checkbook to your bank statement.

As following these rules becomes second nature, you can begin to use your checkbook to record what the payment was for and to mark off whether it is tax deductible. (Make a short list on the front cover of your checkbook record of those items that are tax deductible, then code those payments that apply.) But don't worry about that at the beginning. Just record the check and the amount.

Reconciling a checkbook to a bank statement is probably the key reason people (Messies and Cleanies) develop phobias about personal finance. I can't give you a step-by-step guide on how to reconcile your statement, but I can give you a few tips as you begin to puzzle out your own system.

1. Invest in a small printing calculator, one that uses a paper tape. Using a calculator makes the job of keeping a running balance much easier and the tape makes it possible to double check your work (yes, double check). You won't be as inclined to put off doing your arithmetic and you can easily take advantage of little minutes to catch up.

2. Don't forget to deduct fees. Many a balancer has been reduced to tears for spending the money that the bank already spent. Better yet, find a bank with free checking.

3. On the back of most check bank statements is a form to fill out to help you reconcile your account. Provided it isn't in finance-ese, this can often be a help in learning how it should be done.

4. If controlling one large checking account every month is too awesome, consider using two accounts, one for fixed expenses and one for flexible expenses. Into the fixed expenses account goes the money for the rent or mortgage, utilities, insurance, and car payments. These have been totaled for the year then divided by the number of paychecks that you receive in a year. The same amount of money comes out of every paycheck and goes into the fixed expense account. Then the funds are always there. If you get an interest-bearing account, you can even earn money while you're at it.

The flexible expense account covers living expenses and special purchases.

The point is this: Reconciling your checking account is very important in the fight to restore order. It is imperative. Unless you do, you can't hope to face *Reality #2: You must keep records.*

By records, I mean copies of paid bills, insurance policies, cancelled checks, deposit records, any piece of paper that has to do with finances. Obviously, some people keep *everything,* but most people are selective.

The reasons that records are necessary are:

1. Records make it possible to plan for the future. By knowing how we spent our money, we can plan for those expenses for the future, refining our spending habits so that we can achieve special goals, like vacations or college educations.

2. Records are necessary for preparing your taxes.

3. Records are to a certain extent required by law. Not the everyday receipts but certain records should be kept for five years. After that, you can't be audited, so then any record that does not relate to your future financial planning can be thrown out. Check with a local accountant to find out what records should be kept and for what length of time.

There are many systems for keeping records. Some are very complicated; some are not so complicated. A few basics include

For filing the monthly bills: An expanding 10×12 file.
You will need to label the pockets yourself.

For cancelled checks, bank statements, deposit slips:
A 5×11 paper file, with a flap.

For those items that you only deal with once or twice a year: Manila folders, suitably labeled.

To hold all of the above: A file drawer or cardboard file box.

By having a few simple tools and a special place to store them, you will manage to control the paperwork. Be certain that your file drawer or box is easily accessible. This means don't use the drawer in the bottom of the refrigerator or use the file as a base for a coffee table. Nothing discourages a system more than not being able to get to it. And be sure to clean out the files at the end of the year. Put all the papers together, first to be used for taxes, then to be bound, labeled, and stored.

Keeping records also means tracking cash expenditures. (This is advanced material, so read accordingly.) You will not be able to plan accurately unless you track how you already spend. This could mean marking purchases in your datebook or in a journal or on a wall calendar. The idea isn't to drive yourself crazy; the idea is to be free to use your money for the things you really want.

Let me tell you where I am in this money odyssey. Last year I hired a bookkeeper, Tina, to keep our personal records for our checking account. She divided the expenses into categories for each month. She balanced the checkbook, too. At the end of the year she summarized them for us. What a revelation that was! I never knew we spent our money like that! Do you know we spent—well, I'm not going to tell you exactly!—on our pets, and that didn't include dog and cat food. Of course our dog did break both his front legs (What an ordeal!) and our horse did develop colic (which can be fatal in horses) and needed the vet several times. Seeing how it added up in yearly terms was shocking. Several other categories were surprises, too.

Looking at our yearly totals, I discovered a large amount unaccounted for by any records. This was money we had taken out of the bank for miscellaneous expenses that we had no record for. To solve that problem, my husband and I are carrying around little books to record cash spending. I'll put those in a cash-only ledger book to see where the money goes and then with headings like Tina's check-ledger book, we'll really know where all the money goes. Each month I'll add the cash and the checks for each category for a record of total spending.

All of this record keeping is absolutely necessary. I could never have handled it five years ago. Back then my life and house were in such a jumble that even keeping up the little book would have been too much extra effort, and not losing the bank statement any month for a whole year would have been impossible, I am sure. It may be too much for you right now if you have trouble finding your shoes and keys on a regular basis. Just as soon as you begin to get your life under control, work on the money part, too. Maybe you are ready now. If so, get busy tracing the flow of that money.

And having faced Reality #1 and #2, you can face *Reality #3: You must file your taxes.* Some people enjoy the challenge of doing their own tax returns. Others really prefer to have someone else prepare them. This choice is entirely up to you. But either way, if you have been faithful in keeping up your checkbook and in keeping your records in order, preparing taxes will be a simple, nontraumatic experience. Unfortunately, the pain of paying the tax bill is something that no amount of organization can soften.

As these financial realities are faced, you will begin to have enough information and courage to face new challenges like the challenge of budgeting. In and of itself budgeting is no big thrill. But budgeting means that you will be able to

Save—Put away funds for the new living room furniture, a special trip, or the swimming pool.

Give—You will be able to regularly support those causes that are near to your heart.

Plan—You and your family will be able to achieve goals that until now you only dreamed about.

See, we got through this entire chapter without one chart or diagram. But remember, these are only the basics. So when you feel you're ready, you can expand and refine your financial savvy by reading (*see* Appendix) or attending classes.

And your rewards? In addition to the peace of mind that you've attained from knowing everything is in order, you will most certainly enjoy the bonus of extra dollars—money you've saved by not bouncing checks and by earning interest on your savings and investments. And if you catch yourself in the mirror with a smug, self-satisfied smile, remember ol' Duke Wayne. "Ya did good, little missy."

14

Photo Albums

If a picture is worth a thousand words, what's a negative worth?

SANDRA FELTON

When a reforming Messie begins the long and gratifying job of pulling the house into order by using the Mount Vernon method, frequently one of the things she finds is that there are packets of photographs to be found everywhere. They are in the desk drawer in the living room. They are in the bedroom drawer. They are on a closet shelf. Many times the industrious Messie also finds undeveloped cartridges of film.

Now the problem begins. We are forced to devise a plan to handle this avalanche of photos. This is an especially difficult job because what we are dealing with here are more than pieces of paper—they are memories, memories of our families. They are pieces of our lives and times, caught and frozen. These times and events will never come again. In short, our photos are personal, irreplaceable treasures. And we are the caretakers of these invaluable jewels.

So we come to the job of preserving and showing them weighted down with responsibility. And there are two tremendous obstacles in the way of our success.

1. The photos are not found in any order. Some are so old that we can't even remember the year or the people. Of course, the undeveloped cartridges must be developed before we can even begin to see what era they are from.

2. We are sticklers for order. When we finish putting in our photos we want to be assured that they are in perfect chronological order. Once we have gone around the entire house and gathered all of our photos into one box and spent our life savings on getting the film developed, we are still reluctant to begin. Why? Because we suspect that maybe, somewhere, undiscovered there is one package we overlooked. If we were to get our book all set up and then find that package, we would have to go back and try to rearrange all the pictures to fit that batch in. This would be a tremendous job. Would it not be better to wait to be sure that there are no other packages, we reason. AND PROCRASTINATION IS BORN. Its mother is perfectionism.

Take heart! There is hope! Here are the steps to follow to set up even the biggest challenge.

I will assume that you have collected up all of the pictures that you know about. (When I did the Mount Vernon method and thought I had them all, I found out that my husband had a cache stashed away in his desk, the one place I had not Mount Vernoned.) If you have overlooked one, don't worry. Begin anyway. I'll tell you how to solve that problem later.

First you need to go to the store and buy the photo album. Buy several at the same time if you think you'll need several. Buy the biggest ones you can find and make sure they have loose-leaf three-ring binder rings like a school notebook has. The pages that fit into the rings should have a clear plastic sheet which covers the photos once they are placed on the photo album page. They will usually adhere lightly when placed on the page under the clear plastic cover. Take along a couple of your snapshots when you go shopping: one vertical shot and one horizontal shot so that you can see how they would fit together on the page. The pages of some albums are just a little too short to take two vertical photos or a little too narrow to hold your horizontal ones. You would have nothing but frustration if you were to get home and find that the pages of your photo album did not quite jibe with your size snapshots.

The next step is to find some nice quiet time when you can go through your snapshots looking for clues as to when they were taken. DON'T take them out of the original packages because sometimes the date is stamped on the package or you have a receipt in there that will help you guess the date. Too often the date doesn't include the year but look for it anyway.

Now the real work begins. Go through the packets of snapshots, putting them as best you can in chronological order out on a table. The size of the children, the size of the trees in your yard, the presence of people who have since moved away or died—these are all helpful clues. If you have moved and have different houses in the pictures, that is a BIG help, of course. Birthday cakes are helpful. Sometimes you can count the candles or you may have put the actual number of the birthday on the cake.

Once you have them somewhat in order, begin putting them in the book. Happily move along at an even pace. Put little tags with the dates and occasions as you go. I use pieces cut from three-by-five-inch cards for the information tags, since you can't write directly on the album page.

Don't let anybody know I said this, but sometimes you can actually cut a photo to the benefit of the album. The background or empty space to the side doesn't need to be included if the snapshot will fit better without it. Ignore your husband, children, or others in the background who are calling to you, "Are you sure you are putting those in the right order?" and "You are not *cutting* those snapshots, are you?" Smile and say, "I know what I'm doing. It's going to be great."

Now, what *does* happen if your worst fears are realized and you do find you have left out something from its proper space? *That's* what the loose-leaf pages are for. You simply take a blank page from the back of the album, put it in the spot where the left-out packet should have been, and you've got it back in order again. The *loose-leaf* pages are the key to the problem of keeping your photos in the proper order.

Try to get the whole job done in one swipe because you have all of the snapshots out and in certain spots on the table. You may have to do it in two sessions if you get worn out by all the decision making. (In which case, please put the things away so the house won't be cluttered. I know you're going to get right back to it tomorrow, but you don't really want the table all junky for that long, do you?)

One more word is necessary. There will be some snapshots that are not worth putting in the book. In that case, *don't*. Throw them away if you can or put them in a shoe box labeled *Discarded Snapshots.*

In order to avoid this problem in the future, try to keep shorter accounts with your photo album. Put your snapshots in shortly after they are taken. Now I always put the number of the birthday on the cake. (*Happy 16th Birthday, Doug.*) We also bought a camera that automatically records the date on each picture.

What to do with the negatives? Very big question. Some people rarely ever have prints made from a negative. Even so, throwing negatives away takes a hardier soul than most Messies have. In fact, such people are probably not Messies at all. The primary rule with negatives is "Handle with Care," which means handle as little as possible. Scratches come easily and cannot be repaired. To store negatives, get a supply of glassine envelopes at an art or photo supply store. Get the long size, designed to hold strips of negatives. Put the negatives for each roll in a sleeve (there will be more than one strip per sleeve), then label the sleeve with the date and event(s) of the pictures. If you're really ambitious, you can add the page numbers on which the photographs are mounted in the album. But the date and event should be enough to help you find the negative you want. The filled sleeves can in turn be organized, labeled, and bound with a rubber band to be stored with your "Discarded Snapshots" box. (Now labeled "Discarded Snapshots and Negatives.") Or you can buy one of those plastic pencil cases with a zipper that fit into a ring binder. Put the filled negative sleeves in the pencil case and put the pencil case in the binder after the last page of photographs.

You've done a big job. Why not reward yourself and include those you love in the celebration? Have a special cookout with the albums as the guests of honor to be shown off. You have done a very special thing. Congratulations.

15

Making Up The Bed

"When you make your bed you get a star."

RUTH KRAUSS
(A Hole Is to Dig)

An absolute *must* right from the beginning of the M.A. program is the daily making of the bed. If a person says that she does not see the need for making the bed daily, she will not succeed in changing her housekeeping ways.

The main reason given is this:

"I go to work early and I don't return until dinner time. I'm not home all day so why make the bed?"

This remark indicates several characteristics which will scuttle housekeeping success.

1. Lack of dedication to beauty and order for the sake of beauty and order. Any person, Messie or not, who doesn't care if they dress in a bedroom with an unmade bed, who can work away from home knowing the bed is unmade, and who can come home to an unmade bed, lacks enough of the spark of caring to get going in the right direction.

2. Poor planning and use of time. It takes one or two minutes to make up a bed. If a person feels she can't take one or two minutes to do a job as important and as rewarding as making up a bed, she won't have committed time for *any* housework. Oh, she may work on jobs that demand it, like washing the dishes so she can eat the next meal, but only emergencies will be done. Only the head will be out of the water.

3. Lack of willingness to change habits. If anything is true of Messies turning into Cleanies it is that there must be some definite habit changes. We may have to get up earlier or read the paper less or make the lunches at night or *something* to make things different, but we will have to change. Otherwise we remain the same frustrated Messies. The bed should be made as soon as it is empty. There are several problems with this approach. They usually involve the husband. Here are certain principles.

IF YOU SLEEP ALONE or get up last—begin to make the bed while you are still in it, straightening the sheets and corners from underneath with your arms and legs.

IF YOU TWO GET UP TOGETHER—make the bed together. He usually won't mind. It seems only fair.

IF YOU GET UP BEFORE HIM—either he can make it or you can, as soon as you reenter the room. Or, make up your side only. He can do his when he gets up.

IF YOU LEAVE BEFORE HE GETS OUT OF BED—in this case, he should make the bed. Do I hear you shouting, "But he will never do it!" Maybe he won't, but as the house becomes nicer and nicer, you'll be surprised at how enthusiastic the family—in this case, husband—will become about maintaining the "niceness."

There are other problems, like people who nap in the afternoon or who have different schedules where one sleeps at night and the other in the day. But let's make a general rule: When the bed is not occupied—no matter for how long—it will be made.

Now let's get down to the actual bed making.

Don't let bed making become a huge project. Every little wrinkle doesn't need to be absolutely smooth. Both sides don't need to be *exactly even. Just make it!*

Now as a further incentive, buy new sheets and a spread if you can. Beauty inspires enthusiasm. One further word: If the bedroom is a shambles, there is not as much incentive to make the bed because the beautiful effect is lost in the clutter. Plus, you and I know how hard it is to make the bed when we can't get close to the side of the bed because of all the books and papers cluttering the floor.

Now for commitment time. Check one below.

☐ I already make my bed each day. That's one thing I do right. Thank the Lord!

☐ Yes! Yes! I will start making the bed just as soon as it is empty each day. I can't wait to get up in the morning so I can begin!

☐ No, I don't believe I will make the bed up. It's not important to me. I like things the way they are.

16

To Work or Not to Work

Many women have already answered the question of whether to work or not in the affirmative. Single women, married women without children, single moms, and moms in two-career families make up a tremendous working force of women. Many of these working women are Messies who have added the time and effort of work outside the home to their already flustered lives.

Maria is a new member of the working force. Like many Messies, she was discouraged by the constant losing battle she fought with the house after she married. She finds it a relief to get up, get dressed, and get away from the clutter each day. Her job away from home is certainly more pleasant and fulfilling than the jumbled and harried existence she was leading. When she returns home at night, the Messie lifestyle is still stressful but at least it is short-lived. Maria is also thinking about getting a maid as soon as she gets things in good enough order for a maid to come, if she can find someone reliable and honest. It's too early to tell how her husband is going to adjust to this whole new way of life.

Maria is not a unique case. Fifty-three percent of all American women are in the work force today. An even higher number, 60 percent, of mothers with children under eighteen work outside the home.

Obviously, there are great variations in how women feel about their working. Twenty-five percent work primarily for personal satisfaction and 15 percent work for economic reasons. The majority of women feel their working has been beneficial to themselves and their families. But there are tremendous stresses along the way. By far the biggest stress for a working mom is lack of time to relate to her husband and, especially, to her children.

No one can have it all. Women today can have part of both a family life and professional life, but not all of the benefits of both. How well the trade-offs work between the two is important.

Sometimes, in the case of many single women who are their own and their children's sole support, the matter of trade-offs is beside the point. Survival is the top priority.

In cases where there is enough money being made by the husband or the husband-wife combination, women do have choices that can make working outside the home more satisfactory all around.

I have had to make those choices, as has every working woman. When I was first married, I had no job skills. It was a frightening thing to feel that I could not support myself or help my family if I needed to because I was not qualified to do anything. When my children were two and three and a baby was on the way (what timing!), I went back to school. I went to the local university only to inquire about taking some undergraduate courses. Through a wonderful set of surprising circumstances, I entered, instead, the master's program in education with a fellowship. This meant I didn't have to pay tuition. In addition, they paid me a stipend to attend school full-time. My husband was able to stay home with the children when I went to school in the afternoon and at night. We had a wonderful pediatrician who said she would make house calls if I was away at school with our only car when a child was ill. Sickness of a child is a big problem for moms who work or go to school.

By the way, there are two hospitals in Iowa where working parents can drop their sick children off for two dollars an hour. This is a lot better than the child staying home alone while sick or being sent to school sick. But I remember how much I appreciated my own mother's love and care as a sick child. It built a bond between us.

When I graduated, I took a part-time job with a private educational clinic. My baby went to be with a close-by, long-established, grandmotherly church woman who had him as the only child she took care of.

My older children went to nursery school. I had a lot of time at home with the children since I worked only twenty-four hours a week. I held and enjoyed that job for about six years. I eventually felt I had to quit it, however, because it required that I work part of the summer. This meant my children were left at home part of the day without the supervision they needed. Too much time with too little guidance.

So I quit. I began teaching instead in a private school which my children also attended. This was just about ideal because we went to and came home from school together, and we had the same vacation off. I recommend teaching as one great career for moms.

My children are grown now. The "baby" is seventeen. The work of Messies Anonymous demands time, effort, and trips out of town. Even so, the family priorities are just that—*priorities*. I adjust my career for the family.

This adjusting of career for family is not just a feminine characteristic. Dr. James Dobson, the well-known psychologist, told me that he was so busy traveling and telling others how to run their families that he was neglecting his own. So he completely adjusted his type of outreach to stay in town for his family's sake.

As previously mentioned, Gordon McDonald, a minister with an erratic schedule, tells in his book, *Ordering Your Private World* (Thomas Nelson, 1983), that he schedules blocks of time for his family long before any other demands can be made on it.

In his book *Your Money Matters* (Bethany Fellowship, 1980), Malcolm MacGregor, a financial counselor, tells of canceling two appointments with important clients to attend a function important to one of his children. The clients were not pleased when he did, I might add.

Because I am not the sole support of my family, I have been able to make big adjustments for my children's sakes. I have also enjoyed working. It got me away from the house and provided interesting stimulation. For most of those years I lived as a Messie and our home was not pleasant from that standpoint. It would not have been any better if I had stayed home, however, because I didn't know how to make it different.

I don't know how women with families work a forty-hour week, and more, regularly.

From time to time I have a week of nine-to-five jury duty downtown. I find that during these weeks I cannot get much of anything done. We go on emergency alert at home. My husband buys TV Dinners, I (exhausted) go to bed early, the cleaning waits, and so on. I guess if I had a regular nine-to-five job, I would adjust. At this point, however, I don't see how I could do it. I don't see how any woman can keep a full-time job and do it satisfactorily. But many do. Many have jobs that require overtime work, as well. A full-time working woman with a family has the most stressful setup in our society today.

Let me add while we are talking about the children that finding a good place for them while Mom is at work is a major consideration.

How can we be sure that the baby-sitter doesn't spend much of her time on the phone with the kids planted in front of the TV? How can we be sure the sitter teaches our children the values we feel are important?

In my area, at this moment, a couple is in jail awaiting trial for abusing several young children in their baby-sitting service in one of the loveliest parts of town. This is an extreme case and certainly the exception. But when it comes to our children, can we be too careful?

Let us assume that the day-care arrangement we choose for our children is safe. How good is safe day-care for children? Opinions vary. "There is no hard evidence that day-care has a negative effect," says one expert. Another says, "If parents anticipate not providing enough time for one-to-one con-

141

tact in the first three years, they should consider not having a child at all."

Brenda Hunter, author of *Where Have All the Mothers Gone?* (Zondervan), cites the only long-term study done on the effects of day-care. These findings were largely negative. Boys raised in substitute care were less interested in schoolwork, more aggressive, and more nonconforming. Girls in substitute care were less well-adjusted and less happy with their childhoods.

Most agree that there are differences between children raised in substitute care and those raised at home. Not all agree as to what these differences are. Those of us who have children need to be careful in assuming that substitute care will not adversely affect our children.

For the mother who absolutely must work, the only alternative is to find the best possible day-care she can afford.

For those who have a choice, the decision to work must be made carefully with the children's welfare in view. What greater priority or privilege can we have than the raising of our children?

There are other circumstances about working to consider as well. We need time to ourselves—time to think, time to read, to dream, and plan. Time to do our nails. Time to enjoy being alive and special.

We need time for our husbands. The majority of working women feel they don't have nearly enough time for their husbands.

We need time for chores and the house. This is a major consideration for a Messie, especially one who wants to reform. When women work, housekeeping becomes more of a conflict in the family than ever. Working women want their husbands to help more with home responsibilities than the husbands want to. Only about a third of working women consider that they have support from their husbands in running the house, marketing, and meal preparation, according to the book *Mothers Who Work* (Jeanne Bodin and Bonnie Mitelman, Ballantine, 1983). Twenty-seven percent of husbands help with cleaning. That means, of course, that 73 percent do not help with the cleaning. It is generally agreed that husbands today are thinking about helping more around the house than they have done in the past. They are approving in principle of men helping their wives in the house. Some younger men may actually be helping more around the house because *their* moms worked, leaving them to do household chores as kids. Men who marry later and have lived alone also tend to help more around the house. In general, however, the housework remains largely the domain and responsibility of the woman. Not much has really changed.

I know a young woman who wanted to go to work as a church secretary to bring in extra income for her family. Her husband said he would let her work on the condition she not let down in any way in her care of the children, house, and himself. Meticulously, she worked and did it all. No compromises or trade-offs for her. The last I heard, she was rushed to the hospital with a bleeding ulcer.

Because of the tremendous pressures, Messies, especially Messies who work outside the home, must put the principles of Messies Anonymous to work for them. We must set goals, dream dreams for the house, overcome procrastination, get control of our "collecting" tendencies, discipline ourselves in the use of time, and use the housekeeping skills that work for others. We must carefully set our priorities since we can't have it all.

There are many ways to approach the problem of working outside the home. Some women feel their primary job is to nurture. They are nurturers. Agatha Christie somehow sandwiched her writing into private little pockets of time when she didn't have anything else pressing from the family. Her family and friends apparently didn't realize she was writing at all because her work did not interfere with her homelife. Once she did take off from her volunteer hospital work to write day and night for three days and complete a book in one giant effort. She was basically a nurturer.

Other women base their work on being partners, not nurturers. Some take it to extremes. A couple, we'll call them the Thompsons, plan to live two thousand miles apart because she has been transferred to a new job location. One lives in Miami, Florida, the other in St. Paul, Minnesota. They plan to meet twice a month in cities and resorts easily accessible from Miami and St. Paul and to vacation together. They are long-distance partners.

Yet other women see themselves as providers. The provider places her job as a top priority as support for the family.

Most of us who work are a combination of these. We are nurturer/partner/providers. This can be rewarding but it must be done carefully to be sure that the partner/provider doesn't squeeze out the nurturer.

In the end the decision rests with you and your family. How do you see yourself? You can do it well *if* you keep it organized and set your priorities at the start.

Search and Destroy— Dejunking as the Ultimate Test

"Every day I'll throw something away, and I'll soon feel better and better."

Motto, Pack Rats Anonymous
PEG BRACKEN

In Messies Anonymous, we like to use kind and gentle words. We don't say *slobs,* we say *Messies.* We don't say *pack rat,* we say *collector,* and we don't say *junk,* we say *stuff.*

Maybe in the case of clutter we should vary our ways and use stronger language. Maybe we should tell it like it is and say *junk.* Let's get vicious on this subject. Clutter has brought more frustration, grief, embarrassment, and strain to people's lives than any other single aspect of Messiedom. No other single problem has so assaulted the dignity and self-esteem of its owners. While clutter is mauling our lives, we are loving it and dragging more of it into our homes. Are we masochists? Do we love to suffer? Why do we do this to ourselves? Is it really so bad? What can we do about it?

Why Do We Keep It?

There are some very good reasons for collecting junk—or so we tell ourselves. We have certain characteristics that make us want to save. We are—

Intellectual. Newspapers, books, college notes—who knows what these

145

might contain or when we might use them? We definitely *must* keep these items.

When doing the Mount Vernon method on my house, I decided reluctantly to let many of my college texts go. Proudly, I took them to a bookstore that bought used books. They were to be privileged to have them if they gave me a good enough price. What a disappointment I was in for. They didn't want them, even if I *gave* them away. Old college texts are pretty useless and, in many fields, quickly out of date. I ended up giving them to the Salvation Army. In the past, books were made to last both in binding and content. Now, however, many books are printed in bulk on inferior paper with paper covers. They are meant to be used and discarded, like Kleenex. Let the libraries do the storing. Magazines are the same.

Not long ago, a friend of mine told me that she had seen my picture in a magazine, which she had received the day before in the mail.

"Did you see the article on vacations in English castles in that same issue?" I asked her.

"No, I missed that. Too bad. I've already thrown the magazine away. I don't like things to pile up." Happily she walked away leaving me in shock. One day! And the magazine was gone. How could she? Messies think: *Cleanies must be mentally dull.*

Creative. Messies love to find unusual uses for clutter. Empty spools can be used to make a toy for baby to play with. Milk cartons can be used for planters. *Reader's Digest* pages can be folded down, sprayed, and made to look like a Christmas tree.

"Let's save our spools, milk cartons, and *Reader's Digests* just in case we have time to do any of these projects," we say to ourselves. Cleanies throw the junk out. Messies think: *Cleanies must be very unimaginative.*

Careful. One of the reasons Messies keep things is because they might need them in the future, "Just as soon as I throw anything out, I need it the next day," we often say.

That's what happens, too. The next day we do find a use for it and say to ourselves, *I knew I should have kept it.*

Sometimes we think this way deliberately. After it's gone, we decide to teach ourselves a lesson. So we find some use for the recently discarded item. We sort of punish ourselves for letting it go. That discourages us from throwing things out in the future.

Sometimes we need some lipstick fast and we find an old almost used up tube that we can dip our little finger into to get some color. Sometimes we can supply the day-care center with egg cartons to make caterpillars with. We then confirm to ourselves, *I am right to keep things.* The truth is that the few times these things come in handy do not make up for the long-term distress of living with junk. Besides, if we lived in an orderly way, we'd know where the good lipsticks were to begin with.

It is inconvenient to need a discarded item, but it is much more inconvenient to live with scores of kept items that we might someday need. Messies think: *Cleanies do not adequately prepare for the future.*

Frugal. There is an old Greek story about a crippled man who begged a strong healthy man to carry him across the river. The healthy man agreed and the crippled man jumped on his back. When the two reached the other side, the crippled man would not get down. He clung so tightly, it was impossible to get him loose. For the rest of his life the healthy man paid for his kind decision to do the crippled man a favor. He carried him for life.

That's the way it is with our belongings. Once we buy them and let them into the house, they won't let go. They cling for life.

Those shoes that give us blisters (but cost so much), that vacuum that doesn't work but might someday if we ever do something about it, the home computer that no one knows how to use ("But they do say they are the thing of the future")—these all cost us money. We must keep them for life no matter how great a burden they are to us in order to justify the rightness of our purchase. Messies think: *Cleanies will throw away good stuff. They don't appreciate the value of things.*

Capable. Messies are very capable people in many ways. One reason clutter sneaks up on them is because they feel that they can handle it. At least that's what they think at first. Even when it is obvious to all others that the junk is out of control, Messies keep saying,

- "I can handle it just as soon as I get enough time."
- "I'll build another room."
- "We'll get a shed."
- "I'll rearrange the basement."

Messies think: *Cleanies don't have the ability to handle stuff like I do. They have to throw it away. I can handle it.*

Appreciative of good things. I gave away my family's cast-iron skillet. It is traditional for my family to use a cast-iron skillet to make corn bread. One skillet had been in the family for years. It *was* a great skillet. They don't make skillets that heavy anymore.

However, I really prefer to make corn bread in muffin pans, myself. I had no use for an iron skillet. Besides, iron skillets are a nuisance to clean. The one I gave away was a good skillet but not good for me. Messies think: *Cleanies don't appreciate good things.*

Helpful. "Someone may need these," we say, tucking the stocking with runs into our old stocking bag. "Perhaps to stuff a pillow. Stockings are hypoallergenic, you know."

"Someone may need these," we say, saving the attachments to the vacuum we are discarding because it is worn out.

So our house is full of old stockings, old vacuum attachments, and old everything else saved forever because we want to be helpful. Messies think: *Cleanies don't think of others enough.*

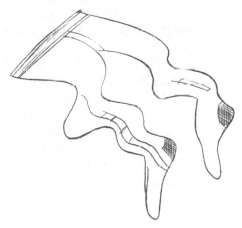

Sentimental. "Aunt Maude gave this to me on my tenth birthday."

"Oh, look, my bathing suit from the summer I was sixteen."

Or the hardest one of all—

"This was Mom's. She left all of her things to me."

Much clutter is the result of inheritance. It must be dealt with in the light of our present needs, not the past sentiment. Messies think: *Cleanies don't value the past.*

Hopeful. One thing that has shocked me into reality is that the things I have kept and valued are not wanted by other people. I always think that things are more valuable than they are. Some things *do* increase in value. Get the facts. *Know* that what you are gathering has a good chance of becoming valuable someday. Chances are that you are fooling yourself into thinking that upon your death, your family will be thrilled to come across some first-rate find. They will have it appraised and say, "What a smart person Mom was to keep this. It has become so valuable." Probably not. If you do decide to collect something for an investment, get some expert opinion now. Expert opinion certainly has opened my eyes. I have gone into a store with a box of treasures and walked out with that same box—the treasures now junk. I was sadder but wiser. All that saving for nothing. Messies think: *Cleanies don't realize how valuable things you save may become.*

So we go about rationalizing how right we are to gather junk and how wrong Cleanies are not to. Our lives are frazzled and frustrated. Theirs are orderly and peaceful, at least as far as the house is concerned.

For Messies, getting rid of our clutter is complicated by our tendency to mix ourselves with what we own. All these things are proof that we have lived a busy, full life. When Messies give things away, we feel as if we've lost a part of ourselves.

Those who surround themselves with clutter, frequently do so to show their worth. They collect the "in" things, even if they don't use them. If they are in the jogging crowd, they have jogging shoes, clothes, and gadgets even if they seldom jog. If they are in the sewing crowd, they have boxes of cloth and patterns, even if they haven't sewn in a long time. Some Messies keep a musical instrument they haven't played in years, or never even learned to play. These symbols show that the owners are joggers, seamstresses, or musicians, whether or not they jog, sew, or play music. This makes the Messies feel better about themselves. They feel more capable.

In another way, however, it makes the Messies feel worse. The unused jogging clothes, sewing material, or instruments put added pressure on the owners. They vow they will get to these things someday. In the meantime, their self-esteem drops lower because they are putting off one more thing.

I remember when I came to grips with the fact that I am not a seamstress. I have had two bouts of sewing fever in my life but recovered quickly from both. I think it is a nice thing for people to sew. It is an admirable activity, but I finally realized that it was not for me. When I came to grips with this sad truth about myself, I gave away two large boxes of material. I remember one beautiful piece of green wool with black flecks in it. Those boxes of material were like the crippled man who rode his benefactor's back. When they were gone (Salvation Army again) I was released. It was nice material, but it was nicer when it was gone.

What we need to do is know ourselves and set our own priorities. As long as we try to be everything we admire, we just muddle ourselves down in confusion. Streamline. Let's be willing to face our limitations. Better still, let's set limitations. Decide your priorities and pare down everything else. It may not all come at once. It took me a while before I could face the fact that I didn't really like to sew, even though I wanted to like it. Be comfortable with yourself as you are and live accordingly. And remember, once you begin to rid yourself of clutter, you are going to have to keep it up or it will gather itself back.

Where Does It Come From?

Where does all this clutter come from? Let's pinpoint the source areas so we can be on guard.

1. Hobbies—Equipment and papers such as magazines and instructions.

2. Clubs and organizations—Scouts, P.T.A., C.E.F., Right to Life, and so on.

3. Vacations—Maps, brochures, and souvenirs.

4. Gifts—What do I do with the hillbilly salt and pepper shakers my daughter brought back from Tennessee or the one ceramic tile with a picture of Brasília on it which a missionary from Brazil gave me?

5. Inheritance.

6. Breakage and loss—The cup with the handle broken

off but also saved in case we get to fixing it. Tupperware top with no bottom.

7. **"Worn out but still good"**—Old faded curtains (maybe we can dye them) and old slacks (for around the house).

8. **"Out of style"**—Ties, dress with a skirt too short but maybe we can put another skirt on it, and shoes hardly worn (they hurt).

9. **General paper**—Flyers, ads, work, receipts, magazines, etc.

10. **Kids**—School papers, hobbies, collections, toys, projects (rub-on letters, magazines to cut out, paper).

11. **Religion**—You *can't* throw away religious materials, can you! That's a sacrilege, isn't it?

12. **Home decorating**—Old fake fruit, old artificial flowers, old pictures stored away with or without cracked glass.

Don't confuse collecting with cluttering. Collectors generally show more restraint than clutterers. They are more selective and they don't keep just anything, especially if it is old, broken, or out of style. There are Cleanie collectors. A collection of any kind is tough to maintain, even for Cleanies, especially if it's a collection of trinkets. Joyce, a Cleanie mentioned in *The Messies Manual,* is a collector of all kinds of small animals made of wood, cork, shells, ceramics, and so on. Her husband built shelves in the windows to display them. They were on the mantel. A few were on tables. When they moved from their home of ten years into a smaller home, Joyce had four garage sales. She did not pack her treasures in boxes to be stored under the bed, in the utility room, or in a rented warehouse. She sold great gobs of her collection. When I asked her how she felt about parting with them, she said that to a large extent it was like lifting a burden. Some things she sold she misses now, like a large ceramic hippopotamus and dishes she used to use every day. When she told me that she missed them she sounded matter-of-fact, not distraught or regretful. As I was about to hang up she said that she had been stimulated by our conversation to begin to get rid of some more clothes. They had been given to her but she didn't like them.

"I believe I'll go right now and get those out of my closet," she said happily.

Not everyone can let go as successfully as Joyce. Just today a reforming Messie told me she had done the Mount Vernon method to her house. She had cleared the rooms and packed everything neatly and tightly into the closets. When she opened a closet, stuff fell out.

"I organized my things, but I didn't get rid of them. Should I?" she asked.

While she was talking, another Messie rushed up.

"Are many Messies pack rats?" she asked.

Yes, they are pack rats (we say *gatherers*). To all who ask the question, "Should I get rid of things?" the answer is, "Yes, get rid of a lot more. YES, YES, YES."

Cleanie collectors and Messie collectors vary in degree. Cleanie collectors can and do get rid of things even with regret. Messie collectors must learn to accept the pain of regretfully parting with stuff (shall we say *junk*) for the pleasure of order.

MEMORIES OR KEEPSAKES?

Why do we hold on to keepsakes,
which can rot, be lost, burn, be stolen,
or, get in the way?

Keepsakes are things.
Things become junk if they fail to have
tangible value.

Memories are better than keepsakes.
No one ever stole a memory;
nor lost one.

Keepsakes can occupy space
which may be needed for things of real
value.

Memories are stored in the heart and
mind—
there's always room for another good one.

Wouldn't it be awful if someone were to
deny himself memories
to make room for more keepsakes?

Wouldn't it be a tragedy if someone were
to deny memories
to others
in order to make room for his own keepsakes?

Keepsakes can be stolen, lost, burned.
We need less of them.

Memories are forever;
We can never have too many good ones.
Robert, Texas
Husband of a Messie

155

Peace Talks

PART FOUR

Cleanliness is not next to godliness. It isn't even in the same neighborhood. No one has ever gotten a religious experience out of removing burned-on cheese from the grill of the toaster oven.

ERMA BOMBECK

" . . . You owe it to all of us to get on with what you're good at."

W. H. ARDEN

Guilt is a funny word. According to Webster's dictionary, it can mean, "responsible for a grave breach of conduct." This is judicial guilt. A person may commit a serious crime, say kill a person, and not feel bad about it at all. Some men on death row laugh about their crimes or say their victim deserved to die. They are judicially guilty but they don't feel guilty.

Another definition of *guilt* is, "a *feeling* of culpability, especially for imagined offenses or from a sense of inadequacy." In this case, a person feels as though he has done wrong, whether or not he actually has. This is psychological guilt.

So which is it with Messies? Scores of Messies have written to me saying that *The Messies Manual* lifted such a burden of guilt. Do Messies who feel guilty have real or imagined guilt?

In chapter 5, "Profile of a Messie: The Reasons" we discussed why some people have trouble with organization and others do not. It is generally because of a lack of one or several natural skills such as visual tune in, attention span, memory, and so on.

When these deficits combine to make a person feel inadequate, she reacts with protective devices such as procrastination, perfection, and guilt. All of this further diminishes her ability. After a while, some Messies say, "I don't care," and quit trying to bring beauty and order to the house. They say things like, "I don't care about the house. I have learned to live with it. I have other priorities." They are trying to escape from guilt.

Guilt can come from several sources: our own conscientious attitudes, the expectations of others, an objective standard we don't meet, or any combination of these three. Let's look at these.

1. Personal expectations. Sometimes guilt comes from ourselves. Messies generally feel guilty because things don't "work" right, not because they don't "look" right. When we lose things, don't have clean dishes for supper, or can't invite people over, we face our failure and that causes guilt. It is this frustration and guilt from living in such an unsatisfactory way that first drives most Messies to seek help. The desire for beauty follows after we have found order for our lives.

2. Others' expectations. Other people, like husbands, kids, and parents, expect us to keep a nice house. Some family members suffer silently, some complain, and others leave. It is true that overzealous Cleanies have run family members out of the house by their excessive neatness. But many have fled a house because of messiness, too. A university study found that the subject couples argue about most is not money, sex, or in-laws, but the condition of the house. Marriages have been ruined or greatly weakened by arguments over the mess the house is in. When one partner is a Messie and the other a Cleanie, there usually is a lot of emotional stress between them. However, the Cleanie helps to keep the Messie from going too far down the road to cluttered ruin. This is a plus for the Messie. Opposites do attract because each person seeks the other to balance his or her weaknesses. The Messie woman may be attracted to an orderly man. He may be attracted to her carefree attitude. As long as the differences are not too great and love prevails, it works for the benefit of the Messie's house. Sometimes, however, when the marriage is under stress or the husband is having a hard time at work and needs a peaceful home in which to recuperate, patience wears thin, tempers flare, people say things they don't mean, and the marriage is strained.

A man from Dallas called me to discuss his Messie problems: "I love to collect things. I have rooms full of stuff. I was divorced last year because of my collecting," he explained in a rather detached way. But I wonder how many emotional months or years he and his wife went through before the end. I wonder if he really felt as casual about it as he sounded.

3. Unmet standards. Sometimes we feel guilty because we have violated an important standard. Many suspect they have violated God's law. So then they face two problems. They feel that in addition to having to live in a messy house on earth, they also are under the cloud of heaven's displeasure. God *does* care about our houses, but not in a vengeful way. He cares because He sees us hurting. We are very special to God. Made in His image, we are people of worth. He has a special plan for our lives. It is not right that we should live frustrated, unhappy lives that demean and humiliate us and those who live with us. It is not right that we should be shackled with guilt and frustration which hinder us from being the people God wants us to be. It is precisely because we are made in God's image that messy houses bother us and those we live with. He is a God of order and beauty. We are not happy if we do not have some of that characteristic in our lives, too. So we strive for order. We feel guilt if we fall below whatever standard of orderliness we have set for ourselves.

I don't think we should feel any guilt about our housekeeping at all, not one twinge of guilt.

You do not have to punish yourself because the house is a mess. Frustrated? Yes, that's allowed. Guilty? No.

If you are one of the souls who has, in the past, convinced yourself that you *should* feel guilty about the house, you have a hard habit to break. People who feel guilty about the house, generally feel guilty about a lot of other things, as well. Please set about breaking the guilt habit as soon as possible.

Develop your feelings of worth. Seek out people who build up your self-esteem, who compliment you, who think there is something great about you even if it's not your housekeeping. You have worth whether you believe it or not. No one can give you dignity and worth; but people can take away your feeling of worth. It is your job to bring your feelings into line with reality. You are a person of supreme value. Recapture the joy of that fact.

Perhaps there are already people who value and esteem you, but when they compliment you, you reject the truth of their compliments. Write down all the good things people like about you and accept them even if you can hardly believe they are true.

As I have said in a previous chapter, avoid those who put you down. If you can't avoid them fully, void what they say as much as possible. You are a person of dignity. A person of dignity does not accept put-downs.

Face the area that is degrading your self-esteem. For Messies, the house is a big part of why we feel bad about ourselves. We need to do two things about that:

First, lower your standards of housekeeping. "WHAT!" I hear many screams coming across the nation to my house. "We are reading this book to get help and here this woman is destroying our motivations by telling us to lower our standards!"

Upon reading this, a man who bought this book for his Messie wife, hoping it will help her, is now deciding not to give it to her. *If the housekeeping gets any lower, we'll all have to move out,* he thinks.

Wait before you panic. I said lower your *standards.* Many Messies are paralyzed by unrealistically high standards. We know we can never reach the perfection we want, so we do all kinds of strange compensating that ends up producing a messy house. Overly high standards hinder success. Be more realistic in your goals and your housekeeping will improve.

Second, begin changing the house. Begin easy. Do the Mount Vernon method a little every day, taking one day a week off. Choose a few of the daily jobs on the Flipper to do each day while you are beginning the Mount Vernon method. Just do those two things—the Mount Vernon and the dailies— to get started. When you set up the Flipper System, be gentle on yourself. Don't set up jobs that would take two full-time maids all day to do. As you improve, you can raise your standards to a comfortable level.

Remember those dreams and goals we are keeping in our

minds. Thoughts will reproduce themselves in the physical world automatically. But it does not happen overnight. Your dreams don't have to come true right away to keep from fading. Have confidence in the strength of your dreams. Follow the techniques for keeping up your motivation. Do self-talks, listen to encouraging tapes, and read your goals frequently.

Relax. Don't feel guilty about the house. Begin the change. Don't pay attention if hubby says, "Boy, I bought you that book and I can't see that it's doing you any good!" Just keep going a little at a time. Be relaxed and happy. You don't have to prove your worth by having a spotless house. You are already a person of worth. When you really begin to believe you are a person of dignity, you will have the motivation to continue with the house until it reflects the wonderful person you are. People of dignity do not live in clutter. Therefore, the clutter will go—slowly but very surely. Perhaps then, compliments will come. If so, embrace them. Whether or not anyone compliments you, you'll know when success begins to come. Compliment yourself. Reward yourself.

You can relax because you know your determination is steady.

What will you do about the feelings of guilt because of the unchangeable past? Fight them. When punishing thoughts come to make you feel bad, make them go away. Say just the opposite out loud to yourself even if you don't believe it. Say it often and say it loud.

Why am I so strong against guilt? Because it is unnecessary and unproductive. Guilt saps our energy, discourages our efforts, clouds our goals, and lowers our self-esteem.

Acceptance of ourselves as we are, coupled with a feeling of our own dignity, will clear the path for change. When we see our failures to live up to our standards, we will not berate or accuse ourselves. We will begin, lovingly, to correct our faults. Trust me. Getting control of the house is a big job. We can't afford the time or energy to feel guilty. We've got work to do.

The final blow against guilt is that the closer our performance gets to our standards the less we'll struggle with the feeling of guilt.

As the house becomes more orderly and beautiful, positive feelings of joy and pride will replace it.

You do not need to leave your room. Remain sitting at your table and listen. Do not even listen, simply wait. Do not even wait, be quite still and solitary. The world will freely offer itself to you unmasked, it has no choice, it will roll in ecstasy at your feet.

FRANZ KAFKA

Liberty

(The Joy of Retreat)

An inability to stay quiet . . . is one of the most conspicuous failings of mankind.

WALTER BAGEHOT

The electricity went off today at the school where I teach part-time. The whole city was blacked out. It was time for me to go home but traffic spilling out of the city to escape the inconvenience clogged arteries in which there were no traffic lights working.

Unexpectedly, my life was stalled. Three hours to spend, or rather invest, in something. But what? Devoid of plans or of any way to generate elaborate efforts, I sat in the school library. The air conditioners were off, of course; there was no electricity to run them. We could hear the occasional voices of students at their lessons floating in the windows. We could feel the breeze and barely smell the smoke of the fire that had broken the electricity flow by burning a major cable.

In a library one reads. Without planning, I was alone with book, breeze, and quiet. The blackout was expected to be a long one. The news said it was extensive, covering the entire southern part of the state and involving over three million people. Could I drive home tonight without traffic lights working? Would the plans

Ivan and I had for dinner out and an infrequent movie be canceled? How could I cook tonight if I had to? I pitied people caught in elevators and was glad I was not one of them. The uncertainty of the future contrasted sharply with the serene reading I had been compelled to do in the library. Even the clocks stood still. We had two hours of powerless living.

Then suddenly and unexpectedly, life returned to normal as the power surged back. Students cheered as they turned on the air conditioners and closed the windows. They went back to normal. The library air conditioner, loud and mechanical, replaced the breeze and gentle voices of children outside. Life was indeed back to normal. But how nice it had been to be forced to delay my busy afternoon and float planlessly with nothing to do but what was at hand. Now the clocks and life had started again. What a shame.

Without electricity, I had seized the time with fervor. Lately I have begun to see the value of unpressured time. Time for me alone. Women today are parched for time alone. Not knowing the source of the thirst, we seek satisfaction in distractions. We feel the itch but can't place our hand on the place to scratch. We dissipate ourselves in many activities and can't find a source of renewal. The vague, unsatisfied need remains unsatisfied.

Women are givers. We give ourselves to our husbands and our children, to our obligations. In order to give in a satisfying way, we must have a source of replenishing. Anne Morrow Lindbergh, in her wonderfully insightful book for women, *Gift From the Sea,* reminds us that the more the nursing mother gives the more she has to give. Even she, however, must replenish herself with nourishment.

In pregnancy as well as nursing, we sustain life by the giving of our bodies. This is just a physical aspect of what women do emotionally and in many ways in the lives of those who depend on us. It is not that women resent giving. We resent giving purposelessly. We resent giving without our willingness being considered. We resent giving when we have been expended and our lives have not been replenished. This kind of exchange is not giving, it is just taking.

Modern lives are not geared for replenishing of soul and

spirit. We have gained conveniences but lost graciousness. To turn the tide requires a breaking of old patterns. We must seek a quiet room, a quiet place, a quiet time.

As a child, I was enchanted by a book called *The Secret Garden* by Frances Hodgson Burnett (Dell, 1962). The story is about a sour, lonely, orphaned English girl from India who is transported to a mansion on the moors of England to live. Left pretty much to herself by the servants and her absentee guardian, she finds the key to the hidden door of the secret and mysterious garden which had been locked untended for ten years.

She was *inside* the wonderful garden and she could come through the door under the ivy anytime and she felt as if she had found a world all her own. Alone day after day, tending the neglected garden, it worked its magic on her and later through her on others.

Women today have chosen complicated lives involving food, clothing, activities for ourselves and our children. We have groceries to buy. We have the obligations of swimming lessons, dancing lessons, karate lessons, school functions, and doctor and dentist appointments. When necessary, we need to deal with plumbers and with repairmen who tend to our cars, refrigerators, and washing machines. Then there's the day-to-day maintenance—washing clothes, giving vitamins, fixing meals, buying clothes, sewing on buttons. If we ever have a moment to ourselves, say in the car while returning from dropping the kids off somewhere, we turn on the car radio to fill the void. When we pause to rest in the house, the TV mercifully distracts us from reflecting on the state of our lives. It is a chosen way of life for us. Women who have money enough to hire others to take the burdens of daily living, are just as busy in other kinds of activities as their less wealthy sisters.

America is a busy place.

"It's the American life-style," my friend says emphatically. "When we first returned to America from living in the Dominican Republic, we were so amazed at all that was available in the supermarket and other stores. There was so much. We weren't used to it."

"Did you like it?"

"Yes! At first it was fun. But after a while it was just so much clutter. We missed our more simple life-style."

Comparing the American life-style to the primitive cultures where there is much more leisure and the men maintain their comfortable life-styles with only a few hours of work a day, a sociologist commented, "In highly technical societies, we are sentenced to a life of hard labor."

One of the most thought-provoking statements I have ever read was a simple letter written by a member of our school faculty who had left the busy city life of Miami for a small college town in his native New York.

A marvelously talented mathematician and excellent musician, he had led our school to heights of musical achievement never reached before or since—the choir concerts, the madrigal dinners, the chamber singer! In addition, he sang in the local city opera chorus and gave voice lessons. All of this was in addition to his mathematics teaching schedule.

His wife, a graceful and very capable young woman, busied herself with working full-time as a personal secretary, carrying a crowded piano-teaching schedule in the late afternoons and on Saturday, and caring for two young children. I think she also typed term papers for others.

I cannot tell you how I admired their productivity and efficiency. How highly respected they were. What contributions they made. How we missed them when they left.

The letter they wrote to the school told a bit about their new life in New York State and added, "When we think of the busy lives we lived in Miami, looking back, we wonder why."

Activities, like barnacles on a ship's hull, crowd to fill in any vacant space. There are times, however, when we have a chance to stand back and reflect on our lives and wonder why.

My high school had a school prayer by John Greenleaf Whittier. At that time we prayed freely in public schools. The third verse of the prayer poem was meaningful to me then and speaks our present need so well.

Dear Lord and Father of Mankind

Drop Thy still dews of quietness,
   Till all our strivings cease;
Take from our souls the strain and stress,
   And let our ordered lives confess
The beauty of Thy peace.

JOHN G. WHITTIER

There will always be distractions. None of us, whether big-city-busy, or farm-busy or career-busy, are ever again going to have the responsibility-free life of a child who can spend unlimited time in a secret garden. However, to remain whole, we must find *some* time to spend alone in our secret garden. Perhaps it is a daily hour, a vacation alone, a day by ourselves. Eugene Peterson says it well: "The precedent to quit doing and simply be is divine." Time alone heals, strengthens, soothes, and refreshes.

Since I have a husband who works at home and children living at home, my house is seldom empty. I remember once when they had all left, probably to go visit Grandma at her house on the Florida Keys, and I had stayed home. Forced to be out on an errand, I was talking with a friend at her business. With a sense of urgency, I moved quickly, explaining to her, surprised at my own feelings, "I have to get home. There's nobody there and I have a chance to be alone."

When my children were smaller and more demanding of constant attention (I had three children in five years and the middle boy was hyperactive), occasionally I would fix the family dinner, serve it, and go out to dinner alone. It was not for the food. It was to be able to sit alone and reflect.

My schedule makes many demands on me and means I am with other people too much. Surely it is not this way with everyone. Perhaps it is with most. But do women who are alone more than I am really spend their time alone or do they spend it doing busy things with the TV on? When do we have time to slow down, to think, and to replenish the self?

When we understand the importance of solitude, we will find the time for it. Solitude is not valued by society however. We have to grab bits of it for ourselves if we are to have it. Gordon McDonald schedules time alone in his appointment book and consults his book when he is urged to do something. He says he has the slot scheduled. He does not say, "I need solitude." People wouldn't understand. In *Gift From the Sea*, Anne Lindbergh writes, "But if one says, I cannot come because that is my hour to be alone, one is considered rude, egotistical, or strange. . . . One has to apologize for it, make excuses, hide the fact that one practices it—like a secret vice!" Society admires much more the too-cluttered schedule, the unnecessary errand, the going life.

Too busy, we don't have time to bring order to our homes. Our checkbooks drift because we don't have time. We'll get to the folding of the clothes later—or better still, we'll just use them as we need them out of the basket. Worse than all of this is that our inner world is neglected, and that is so important. Plato once said that the unexamined life is not worth living. Our lives are too busy; plans are forgotten; memories are jumbled; joys are obscured. We are in such a hurry we hardly know who we are, much less how to develop and replenish ourselves.

Diane, a strapping pioneer woman nearing forty, suddenly found her challenges met and her life flat. For the first time, she was depressed and at ends. For Christmas, according to Gail Sheehy in *Pathfinders,* the woman's husband built her a very special gift: a tiny, round peak-roofed bonnet of a dwelling out back—an escape house. Her children's gift was a week for Mom in solitary; they brought her meals, tended the family house, and allowed no one to enter her hut. For seven whole days Diane simply "not did." When she came out, she knew she wanted to go back to school.

Her tomb of solitude became a womb in which she began to grow into a new life. We need solitude in order to grow.

We must stop, reflect, find solitude, take time just to be.

The story is told in the Talmud of a certain Rabbi Zusya. Reflecting on his reason for existence, he once said, "In the coming world, they will not ask me: 'Why were you not Moses?' they will ask me, 'Why were you not Zusya?' "

What about you? What about me? Are we the best Mary, John, or Sandra we can be? Or did we lose ourselves somewhere in the rush?

Whatever is true,
whatever is noble,
whatever is right,
whatever is pure,
whatever is lovely,
whatever is admirable—
if anything is excellent or
praiseworthy—
think about such things.

PHILIPPIANS 4:8 (NIV)

20 | The Pursuit of Happiness

Less is More.
ROBERT BROWNING

How can we pursue the task of becoming the person we were intended to be?

How can we arrive at the point where we can look at our lives, including our houses, and say, "This is me and it is good." This was Rabbi Zusya's goal. We won't stumble across this. It will not come by accident. We must pursue it deliberately.

Seek Simplicity

Truly successful people are those who know how to seek and find simplicity in life. They seek it because simplicity acts as a unifying force which gives meaning to life.

The Messies Anonymous Mount Vernon method is a starting point for finding a more simple life because it helps us thin out the unnecessary clutter of "things." Some people try to reorganize their overabundance. Ladies' magazines encourage this by showing us how to store things in ever-expanding nooks and crannies. They urge storage of junk. Resist the temptation to pack more in tighter. Instead, take the opportunity to get rid of the clutter that complicates our living.

In addition, in order to simplify our lives, we must Mount Vernon our activities, throwing out or giving others some of the activities that jam our lives together into a mass of busyness. By cutting out unnecessary appointments, insignificant errands, and fruitless activities, we free ourselves from pettiness. Be careful not to use time-management techniques to organize your time so that you can crowd more activities in, to pack them tighter. We need to select only the most valuable activities. And these activities we keep can now take on a significance that they once lost in the hurry of our days. When life is rushed, life's activities then become mere "happenings." We must protect ourselves against this. Just as flowers left to grow in a jumble without being thinned out never reach their potential beauty, our lives left unthinned lose vitality and the ability to develop fully. We crowd our lives into mediocrity. We must thin our gardens for maximum beauty.

Seek Nature

Some of us live in beautiful, strengthening environments. Perhaps you only have to step foot on your porch to see the splendor of mountains and valleys below you. Perhaps if you glance out your window you look down on a panorama of azure and aqua ocean, blending in ever-changing, beautiful patterns. Or perhaps you see a placid lake reflecting like a mirror on still and quiet mornings. If so, you have the marvelous privilege of intertwining yourself with nature at a moment's notice. Most of us, however, are not so blessed. We must go out of our way to seek nature if we are to find it. It is imperative for us to do whatever necessary to seek nature's beauty. All people must regularly experience nature in order to develop into what God intended us to be. It was no mistake that Adam and Eve were put in a garden. We humans are made of the stuff of this earth and to it we return. We do not just walk on earth, we *are* earth. If we travel on too much concrete or stare at too many plaster walls without returning to our source of being periodically, we begin to lose the edge of who we are.

In South Florida, as in many other places, we have our problems with seeking out nature. The tropics, like a high-strung horse, are beautiful and exciting but difficult to live with. The heat, the brightness, the overgrowth of plants, the insects, all combine to drive us indoors, away from nature, into air conditioning and behind screens. Those who visit South Florida may feel that the ocean, palm trees, and sun offer a relaxing interlude, but those who live here long begin to feel the loss of the gentleness of the temperate zones.

In order to see and stay in touch with nature, our family has done several things. We bought a house with thirty feet of windows in the living room. Three of these six-foot windows are from ceiling to floor. Outside the windows, my husband has planted an abundance of tropical foliage. Through the windows we hear the birds, the neighborhood noises, and the splat of raindrops on the palm fronds. Strangely enough, as I write, I am being interrupted by a hailstorm as our rainy season begins. White ice marbles are jumping in the green grass as they hit. Nature is full of surprises.

In order to pull myself out into nature on a daily basis, I use a solar clothes dryer (known to some as a clothesline) instead of an automatic dryer. Because I dry my clothes in the outside air, I must go out regularly. I must feel the heat, the cool, the breeze; and I watch the sky for rain. Nature and I work together on drying clothes.

Our house has no built-in heat. For heat in winter, we use the sun and, occasionally, a small plug-in space heater. For coolness, we use fans and trees planted outside. Our bedroom has an air conditioner but it's seldom used.

We like being close to weather changes. In our house, we live *with* the changes, not against them. I am not, for a minute, suggesting that our way is the best for all people who live in the tropics and certainly not the way those in the temperate zones should live. I am only saying that if each of us is not careful in this technological society, we can seal ourselves so far away from nature that we only come out to use it for recreation. We need to enjoy it and live with it, not just use it, in order to develop ourselves fully. Wherever you are, make it a point to make contact with and seek out nature, preferably alone.

As a child, I walked on Arkansas mud. So firm was the consistency that I could actually walk on the mud without it sticking to my feet or squishing up between my toes. It was wonderful. I remember rowing in a Arkansas pond and looking into the mouths of hissing cottonmouth moccasins around the banks. I remember walking in the black, cool waters of a Florida stream.

I don't know why, but I am better today for these experiences; not because they were in the past, but because they are still a part of me today. We need to continue these healing touches.

Seek a Rhythm of Living

Nature has its rhythms of light and dark. It has its lunar month of twenty-eight days. Earth has its rhythm of seasons. We humans have divided our lives into weeks and calendar months and years in some loose cooperation with the rhythms of nature.

God works in rhythms. We see His rhythms in the nature around us. We also see it in creation where He worked six days and rested one. Following His example and injunction, orthodox Jews have strictly kept the sabbath rest one day out of seven. Life achieves a strong weekly rhythm in this way.

Rhythms give meaning to the movement of life. But for some of us the only rhythm kept is work until exhausted, sleep until awakened to work again until exhausted. We hit the floor running, grabbing coffee to stir us into action faster.

This is the pattern of a runaway life-style. Like music played too fast and without rhythm and pauses, we have a cacophony in our living. What we need to do is to set the metronome slower and follow a steady rhythm complete with significant pauses, called in music, rests.

To set up the rhythms of life requires planning. Gandhi planned to spin each day. Bernard Baruch planned to sit on a park bench each day. We must each plan a pattern to fit our temperament and schedule. I like to begin my day with a pause. Being a morning person, I usually awaken naturally about 5:30 A.M. Most often I arise immediately and go to my living room chair where I spend the next hour alone—no TV, no newspapers. I begin by writing in my journal. This starts my mind on a serene path. I read the Bible and occasionally other inspirational books. I think and pray. It is the fastest hour in the day. I keep no schedule for this hour. It is just my hour alone—but not altogether alone at all. As in Michelangelo's picture of the creation of Adam, I reach out my finger and touch that finger from whom all life flows and I am refreshed.

Too soon it ends. I get the family up, read the paper, make the bed, eat, dress, and leave for work. The tempo quickens, but the early-morning pause has given the day significance. Life rushes in clearer, fuller, more vivid than before.

I also observe Sunday as a day of pause. It gives the week rhythm. The Sunday-morning service is the high point of my week. We have a Sunday dinner as a family, when we get home. We rest in the afternoon and in the evening we go to a church function or watch television if no church function is planned. Once a month, our church family eats dinner together on the church grounds. Nothing special presses on Sunday. That's what's special about it.

The church hour has always been a time for a woman to be alone without distractions. An hour of prayer, meditation, instruction, and beauty. She, like each one at the service, stands solitarily before God. It is a time of significance, a time of re-creation. No bustle of children's demands or husband's needs should intrude because it is a special time.

A life with the metronome set too fast will not be able to fully enjoy this pause, however. Even such a significant aspect of life will become just another obligation—not a pause at all. If our lives are full of fruitless activities already, we will grudgingly awake on Sunday morning tired from a busy Saturday. If we awaken late, we will have to rush to the service after griping at the kids (and maybe husbands) to hurry. It takes half the service to unwind and settle down. When it is over, we rush on to more activities made all the more hectic because of the time we took to go to church.

I've lived this life so I know how fruitless it can become.

To make Sunday satisfying, Saturday has got to slow down. To slow Saturday down, we have to control the weekdays. We must force them to march more slowly, in a more stately manner. Only then are the pauses truly "rests."

Seek Beauty

Wherever they are to be found, seek moments of beauty. Many of these moments may be found alone in nature. Sometimes they surprise us as in sunrises and sunsets, sometimes on vacation trips or quiet walks. It is elsewhere, too.

We can make it a point to look for beauty in reading. I love biographies, autobiographies, or informative and inspirational books. Ordinarily biographies are written about people who have much to share. Much beauty is found there.

I wish I enjoyed fiction because exciting truths can be found in fiction. Each of us has his or her own reading interests. Keep reading, including poetry and informational reading which strengthens you. Paperbacks are great. Turn down their page corners. Mark them. Put notations in the margin or the flyleaf. State pages and their significance. One reason I mention so many books is in order to give some guidance in the shoreless sea of books from which to choose. Avoid mediocrity. It is in reading that we find the highlights and shadows that give depth to what would be an otherwise flat existence.

Another source of beauty is music. Perhaps no other area of life has reached such heights of glorious inspiration, and in contrast, such depths of ugliness. You are blessed if you have developed a taste for lovely, inspirational music. If not, try to develop a love for this kind of music. Attend concerts, buy records. Ask friends whose way of life you admire to tell you the music which is meaningful to them and go from there.

What shall we say about television and movies? There is much junk food of soul there. But there is good as well if we care to look for it. Selective viewing can help us find beauty on TV and in movies.

Finally, there is the house. Simplicity does not preclude beauty; it accentuates it. One reason we must get the house under control is in order to place beauty there. Imagine in your mind your house in order and beautifully appointed. How wonderful it is. Living in it, you are beautiful, too. The home reflects loveliness from within you. It reflects loveliness back to you. Seek that finishing beauty in your life, the beauty of your home.

Seek Quality

We can go through the motions of life without those motions being meaningful to others or ourselves. Only as we deliberately seek quality, will life awaken under the fingers of our activities. Rabbi Zusya felt it. Inside yourself you feel the need for quality as well. Then there will be a reason for housework. It will not just be motion. You are reading this book because you seek a quality life.

A student of Pablo Casals, the world-famous cellist, was bowing the cello notes under the master's supervision. Although she was technically accurate, something was missing from her performance, she knew, as she listened to Casals demonstrate those same notes to her. His notes pulsed and glowed from the bow in his hand.

"Bring it to the rainbow," he urged. "Always to the rainbow." Again and again she sought the rainbow and when she found it, joy and music flowed together from within her.

This is our task: to bring the notes of our lives to the rainbow of quality living through finding simplicity of life-style, relating to nature, establishing a satisfying rhythm of life, and enjoying beauty.

Once we feel the joy and pride of that glow, we can never be the same again. And the house? The house will begin to change naturally and surely from the force of the change within us.

Seek simplicity.
Seek nature.
Seek a rhythm of living.
Seek beauty.
Seek quality.

With regard to excellence,
it is not enough to know,
but we must try to have
and use it.

ARISTOTLE

APPENDIXES

MORE ABOUT THIS MESSIE

As I have told the story of how we can all gain control of our houses, I have frequently referred to my own experiences. Perhaps you would like to have a more orderly story of my life to fit things into.

But let me warn you that this story is rated R. The R stands for *Religious*. So if you don't like religious stuff, don't read any further. If you are curious and do read further, don't say I didn't warn you.

For the sake of the story, we will think of life as a trip of sorts. I think of childhood as preparation for the journey we will take—the journey of adulthood.

When we are packing in childhood for the life we will live, we will need to put as many good things in the suitcase of experience as we can. We must try to look ahead to see what we'll need. As on any long trip, we will need almost everything we pack—and more.

When I was young, I packed what I thought I would need. My tastes were rather classic. I took school seriously. I was also tutored in French and in art in addition to my school subjects. Learning was heady stuff for me and I dove in, packing a love of learning into my bag with relish.

Unknown to me, I was packing other things as well. Somewhere along the way, I packed a very strong-willed nature. I also packed a tendency to react poorly to serious problems. That is, I tended to overreact. If my children got sick, I thought they were dying. When anything bad happened, I thought it was disaster. As you can imagine, I had a difficult time coping.

During my childhood, I had a very religious nature. I went to a parochial school, attended church weekly, and tried to follow, seriously, a moral way of life. I supposed that these things would bring me peace with myself and with God. But it didn't work out that way. No matter how good I tried to be, I had no peace in my heart that things were right between God and me. I suspected they weren't. I felt that my sins were not paid for by my "good" behavior. In short, I carried around a lot of unresolved guilt.

About this time my uncle, who had been seeking his own kind of peace in drinking, gambling, success in business, and hobbies, had an experience with God which transformed his life. In sharing this experience with me, he put his finger directly on the problem. In the Bible, there is a verse that says, "Not by works of righteousness which we have done, but according to his mercy he saved us, by the washing of regeneration, and renewing of the Holy Ghost" (Titus 3:5). Another verse says, "For by grace are ye saved through faith; and that not of yourselves: it is the gift of God: Not of works, lest any man should boast" (Ephesians 2:8, 9). So *that* was the problem! God did not absolve our guilt by weighing our good works against our bad ones. I was going down the wrong road and wondering why I didn't arrive at the right place.

So, at the age of thirteen, in the midst of my packing other things in preparation for adulthood, I put into my bag a strong faith in the sufficiency of Christ's death on the cross to "regenerate" and "save" me. And sure enough, when I quit trying to persuade God to save me and just took the salvation He wanted to give, I found that peace I had been looking for. I packed that in, too, and moved on to a different path.

Year after year I packed, and when I got married at the age of twenty-one I started my independent journey. Of course, as we all do, I continued to pick up a few things as I traveled. But on the whole, I lived from the supplies I had already packed away during childhood.

Right away, I started to pull things from that large bag of stubbornness I mentioned earlier. Stubbornness is not a good commodity to bring into a new marriage when two people are trying to learn to live as one together. But there it was.

I also discovered that I had a large bottle of messiness. Its aura permeated the small apartment in which we lived. This was a surprise to me. Up until that time I had lived within my mother's organized and beautifully maintained home. I had assumed maintenance would come easily to me. It did not. Keeping the house under control was a struggle which was to continue for twenty-three years until I found a method that worked for me. Then I started to share it by founding Messies Anonymous. Now as Messies Anonymous continues to grow I am kept busy providing help for Messies through Messies Anonymous. In addition to helps through the mail, the number of seminars held for church and civic groups is increasing. Self-help support groups are catching on and I envision the day when help is available through these support groups whenever Messies seek encouragement in changing their lives.

However, in those early days, I found something else in my bag that I had not known was there. I had not put it in. It had been packed for me. I was born at a time when the medical profession and the world in general was just discovering the power of radiation. Doctors at that time decided it would add extra protection to the health of newborn babies if they gave a heavy dose of radiation to the thymus glands of those babies. I, like many other babies in more advanced hospitals, received this strong radiation exposure. In later years, this caused a serious problem to many of us.

One day as I was sitting on the couch beside my new minister husband, he said, "What's that lump on your neck?"

"You're kidding."

Sure enough there was a lump. The doctor I consulted said that there was no hurry to remove it. I could wait until my teaching was finished in a couple of months. There was no problem.

When the biopsy came back, however, there *was* a problem. It was thyroid cancer. At twenty-one, I was facing what I thought was certain death. My aunt had just died of cancer.

At this time all of the things I had packed were put to the test. The story is told that when a new ship is tested they take it out to sea, go full steam ahead and then shift it into reverse. Whatever is not tightly attached, falls off. That's what happened to me. A lot of things that were not attached fell off.

It was at that time I found in my bag that inability to handle problems which I mentioned earlier. I had not known it was there before. I also found that the strong desire to have my own way made me angry at the Lord, when I thought about the cancer. Why had He done this to me? I threw a tantrum to show Him how angry I was. But I didn't call it a tantrum; I called it depression. So for several years, the worst years of my life, I fought God over what I considered His mistreatment of me. I didn't realize at the time, that it was this anger at God that was causing my depression. When I realized it, I was ready to "forgive" God and to ask Him to forgive me. I was ready to yield my will to His.

It was a surprise to me that I did not die. The cancer did not recur. Time went by. I continued teaching. Children came. We celebrated our silver anniversary. One day I found another lump.

"No." The doctor was reassuring. "It's probably not a problem. It is a soft lump. I'm sure it's nothing. But we should do a mammogram just because it's good to have it done regularly. I'll make an appointment for you at the hospital."

It was cancer again. This time breast cancer. It resulted in a mastectomy. This time I found more good things in my suitcase to meet the crisis than I had found there before. I found more faith in God's will for my life and less desire to have my own way. I held fast to the verse in Genesis 18:25 which says, ". . . Shall not the Judge of all the earth do right?" I found God's peace in the midst of my problems. Maybe I was finally learning a little about how to travel in this life.

We got it early. There has been no recurrence. This incident reminds us of something very important. When we face death, which is what I do each time the doctor finds a life-threatening disease, it is very important to know which road we are on and where it will end. When I die, as we all do eventually, I am happy to know with certainty that my journey will end in my Father's home.

Jesus said: "In my Father's house are many mansions . . . I am the way, the truth, and the life: no man cometh unto the Father but by me" (John 14:2, 6).

I said earlier that this story was rated R. Perhaps it should be rated X for Xtra special and wonderful. Walking with God down the journey makes life so great—so wonderfully, specially, great.

God bless you as you walk this journey along with the rest of us. May your life be rated Xtra special and wonderful, too.

AN ABECEDARIUM FOR MESSIES

Appliances. Beware of appliances. Even when they are "time-saving, easy-to-use," appliances (especially kitchen appliances) have many parts that need cleaning. Many parts also means that there are more things to lose. The time that you save preparing food may be lost keeping the appliance clean and in order. Be tough: If all you need is a knife, use a knife, not a fancy motorized dicer-slicer-peeler-pulverizer.

Books. If you have a large book collection, make the books work for you. Books make great insulation. Put bookshelves on walls that run between rooms to prevent sound from traveling through walls. Great for apartment dwellers. Put bookshelves on the outside walls to help keep the heat inside and the cold outside.

Closets, Cupboards, and Cabinets. Keep them closed. It's amazing how much cleaner a room will look.

Dusting. Always dust with a clean cloth. Better yet, make the *kids* use a clean cloth.

Elbow Grease. Something your mother said would clean everything. Origin unknown.

Fresh Air. Makes any room seem cleaner, somehow. An open window with a fresh breeze beats a commercial air freshener any day.

Gloves. Work gloves can make chores much easier and much more tolerable. They also protect your hands and nails from damage, and you won't get the smell of cleansers imbedded in your hands.

Hooks. Should be on the back of every bedroom door, inside every closet door, and inside the back door or wherever your family dumps their belongings. If you mount hooks at kid height, your children will be able to manage their own coats.

Ironing. Instead of ironing, try using a tailor's steamer on your clothes. Available in most department stores, these hand-held appliances work miracles on most wrinkles. Great for travel as well: lightweight, convenient, much better than a travel iron.

Junk. Be brutal when you have to be. Do you really *need* all those twist ties collecting in your kitchen drawer? If it's junk, name it and treat it accordingly.

Keys. Keep a tray or small hook by the door to hold your keys. Then remember to put the keys there when you come in. And keep a spare set handy.

Lazy Susan. In addition to its traditional use in the refrigerator to hold condiments, a lazy Susan can make any cabinet or cupboad a place of order. For instance, in a spice cupboard or below a sink, or in a workshop or studio. Allows easy access to many things.

Mount Vernon Method. Your personal Declaration of Independence.

Neglect, Don't. Places most often neglected (because you're usually thinking about something else): the bathroom mirror, the telephone, light switch plates, lamp shades, the underside of the lid of a step-on garbage can.

Organizers. Believe it or not, there are people who are professional organizers. They'll organize your closets, your kitchen, your garage—anything. Check the Yellow Pages under "Organizers."

Pot Holders. Nothing makes a kitchen seem cleaner than spotless pot holders. Unfortunately, they don't stay spotless. Wash them often, and know when to give up and buy new ones (toss out the old ones!).

Questions, Ask. If you know a Cleanie (and who doesn't?), ask her how she solved certain housekeeping and organization problems. Even if it's your mother. Don't ask general questions—be specific: "How do you keep the cabinet under the sink in such good order?"

Refrigeration. The reason they tell you not to use sharp objects to de-ice the refrigerator is because a sharp object could easily puncture the wall and a gas line inside the wall. When you puncture a gas line, you have dealt a death blow to your refrigerator. So now you know.

Sheets. Get a different color set for every bed in the house. One set/one bed. When you change the sheets, don't put on a new set and throw the old set in the basement for washing. Wash the set you took off immediately and put it back on the bed it came off of. No folding, no laundry buildup.

Teenagers. Great source of energy. You can hire teens to help you with your yard work and general cleaning for very little money. There are often places you can post cards at local high schools or colleges, if you are looking for help. Be sure you know what you want done, listing specific jobs and the realistic time involved.

Umbrellas. Most Messies despair of ever having umbrellas when they need them. Buy cheap ones. Keep one in the car, one in the office, one in the house. Periodically look around and see if two are in one place. If so, carry one back to its own home.

Volunteer. Not yet. Postpone your volunteer activities until you have your own house in order. Then be selective in your volunteering.

Windows. Washing windows on a dreary winter's day gives you a new outlook on life. There's nothing like getting the dog's nose prints off a big window to make you feel the whole room is clean.

Xerox. Type up a basic grocery list containing all those products you consider absolutely essential to your pantry. Put it in the same order that the store you shop is in. Leave blanks for additional things you will need from time to time. Then Xerox the list. You can check off the things you need, writing your additions in—and off you go.

Yard Sale. Yard sales are to Messies what bakeries are to dieters. Dangerous? Irresistible! So don't go. Or if you must, don't take any money with you.

Zipper-top bags. Great for organizing children's toys that have a million pieces. Also for safekeeping of valuable pieces of hardware your husband has entrusted you with, spare buttons, and so forth.

MORE READING

Aslett, Don.
  Is There Life After Housework? Cincinnati: Writer's Digest
  Books, 1981.
  Do I Dust or Vacuum First? Cincinnati: Writer's Digest
  Books, 1982.
  Clutter's Last Stand. Cincinnati: Writer's Digest Books, 1983.

Casewit, Curtis W. *Diary: A Complete Guide to Journal Writing.* Allen, Tex.: Argus Communications, 1981.

Editors of Consumer Guide. *The Fastest, Cheapest, Best Way
  to Clean Everything.* New York: Fireside, Simon & Schuster,
  1982.

MacDonald, Gordon. *Ordering Your Private World.* Nashville,
  Tenn.: Thomas Nelson Publishers, 1985.

Peterson, Jean Ross. *Organize Your Personal Finances: Turn
  Chaos Into Cash.* Whitehall, Va.: Betterway Publications,
  Inc.

Pinkham, Mary Ellen.
  Mary Ellen's Best of Helpful Hints. New York: Warner
  Books, 1980.
  Mary Ellen's Best of Helpful Hints, Book 2. New York:
  Warner Books, 1981.

Mary Ellen's Best of Helpful Kitchen Hints. New York: Warner Books, 1980.

Mary Ellen's One Thousand New Helpful Hints. New York: Doubleday & Company, 1983.

Rushford, Patricia H. *From Money Mess to Money Management.* Old Tappan, N.J.: Fleming H. Revell Publishers, 1984.

Waitley, Denis E. *Seeds of Greatness: The 10 Best-kept Secrets of Total Success.* Old Tappan, N.J.: Fleming H. Revell Publishers, 1983.

Winston, Stephanie.
Getting Organized. New York: Warner Books, 1980.
Getting Organized: Storage. New York: Warner Books, 1981

Young, Pam, and Jones, Peggy.
Sidetracked Home Executives. New York: Warner Books, 1981.
Sidetracked Sisters Catch-up on the Kitchen. New York: Warner Books, 1983.

To obtain further help from Messies Anonymous, write to:

Messies Anonymous
5025 S.W. 114th Avenue
Miami, FL 33165